Powerful Places in Sintra

Powerful Places in Sintra

The Magical Mountain of the Moon

Elyn Aviva

and

Gary White

Powerful Places in Sintra

The Magical Mountain of the Moon

by

Elyn Aviva & Gary White

Copyright © 2022 by Pilgrims Process Publishers

http://www.PowerfulPlaces.com

The authors and publisher have made every effort to ensure the accuracy of the information in this book at the time of publication. However, they cannot accept responsibility for any loss, injury, or inconvenience resulting from the use of information contained in this book.

ISBN: 978-0-9915267-9-6

Set in Minion Pro 11 pt. and Luminari in various sizes.

Cover photo: Moorish Castle at night

Photo Credits: Elyn Aviva, Sara Daniel (p. ii), Maria João Martinho (p. 120), Jane Seiler Thompson (p. 139), Adobe Stock, and Google Earth, Photo provided by João Paulo Afonso of himself in 1981 as soon-to-be-crowned Emperor (p. 207).

Acknowledgements

First, we acknowledge the power of Sintra. It drew us to it and demanded that we write about it. The Spirit of the Mountain of the Moon is alive and well, for those with eyes to see and ears to hear.

Second, we acknowledge the people who have helped us to learn about Sintra and whose suggestions have improved this book. Thank you, Wannes Debussier and Ana Rute Tomas, for sharing with us some of your favorite places in Sintra and for commenting on the manuscript. We want to thank Margery Leroux, Marchiene Riestra, Melissa Snyder, and Jane Seiler Thompson for their careful proofreading and thoughtful observations. In addition, we are grateful to Maria João Martinho^, Luis Élye^, and Ana Paula Roneberg, who have shared with us their deep knowledge of Sintra, its history, its mysteries, and its esoteric past.

Third, we are grateful to each other for our shared dedication to explore this mysterious multiverse in which we live.

Other Books by Elyn Aviva and Gary White

Powerful Places Guidebooks by Elyn Aviva and Gary White. Listed in alphabetical order.

Powerful Places in Brittany
Powerful Places on the Caminos de Santiago
Powerful Places in Catalonia
Powerful Places in Cornwall and the Isles of Scilly
Powerful Places in Ireland
Powerful Places in Malta: A Broader Perspective
Powerful Places in Scotland
Powerful Places in Wales

Non-Fiction books

The Dowsing Mind—Into the Multi-dimensional Realms and Back. Gary White
Where Heaven and Earth Unite—Powerful Places, Sacred Sites, and You. Ferran Blasco and Elyn Aviva
Following the Milky Way: A Pilgrimage on the Camino de Santiago (2nd Edition). Elyn Aviva
Walking Through Cancer—A Pilgrimage of Gratitude on the Way of Saint James. Elyn Aviva

Fiction

Melita's Quest for the Grail. Elyn Aviva
The Question—A Magical Fable. Elyn Aviva
The Journey—A Novel of Pilgrimage and Spiritual Quest. Elyn Aviva

Contents

Key to Abbreviations

Distances are given both in metric and imperial measures. Both are abbreviated.

cm = centimeter

ft = foot

km = kilometer

m = meter

mi = mile

sq km = square kilometer

sq mi = square mile

Symbols

A * indicates the word is defined in the glossary at the end of the book.

A ^ indicates the person/author is listed in the bibliography at the end of the book.

Titles

Dom and dona are Portuguese titles for nobility and aristocracy, including but not limited to kings and queens. In this guidebook, all the people referred to as dom and dona are kings and queens.

UK
EUROPE
Portugal
France
Italy
Spain
PORTUGAL
Sintra

Part I—Introduction

"Powerful Places Guidebooks" provide detailed information and suggestions for turning casual tourism into transformational travel. There is no better location to include in this series than the UNESCO World Heritage Cultural Landscape Site of Sintra and its magical Mountain of the Moon.

Sintra is not just one place, it is three. Sintra is (1) the name of a small town in western Portugal, just a little north and west of Lisbon; (2) the large municipality that encompasses it; and (3) the low granite massif (also known as the Mountain of the Moon) that rises abruptly out of the plain and stretches 16 km (10 mi) from the town of Sintra to the Atlantic.

Sintra is a unique blend of striking natural landscape, elaborate gardens, and stunning castles and palaces. But more than that, Sintra is a state of mind: open to the unexpected, delighting in the fantastic, and eager to explore the unknown.

> Sintra is not just a place: it's a state of mind.

Sintra is a mysterious, alluring place. Humans—including ancient Paleolithic and Neolithic people, the early Iberians, the Celts, the Phoenicians, the Greeks, the Romans, the Moors, the Knights Templar*, religious communities, Portuguese nobility, and numerous famous writers, musicians, and artists—have been drawn to Sintra for more than 7,000 years.

George Gordon Byron (Lord Byron) called it "a glorious Eden." Richard Strauss thought the Holy Grail Castle was here, on the hill. The poet Robert Southey declared it "the most blessed spot on the whole inhabitable globe." Hans Christian Andersen described it as "the most beautiful place in Portugal." There is so much here—and of such importance—that the area was declared a UNESCO World Heritage Cultural Landscape Site in 1995.

Sintra is a magical symbiosis of nature and human creativity. A marvelous mix of lush parks and wild forests, of hilltops often shrouded in mist, of ruined fortresses, medieval monasteries, and 19th-century fairytale palaces that cast a spell on all who visit. Romantic architecture, extensive parks, arcane symbols, a (perhaps) Masonic initiation well all contribute to the enigmatic otherworldliness that pervades the landscape.

Sintra. Its name may come from the Indo-European *Suntria*, meaning bright star or sun. Or, more likely, it is named for Cynthia, the Greek goddess of the Moon, whose name morphed to Sintra. She was equated with the Greek goddess Artemis, who was equivalent to the Roman goddess Diana. Diana was associated with the hunt, wild animals, childbirth, and the Moon.

"In the universe, there are things that are known, and things that are unknown, and in between, there are doors." —William Blake

Sintra Mountain, also known as the Serra de Sintra and the Mountain of the Moon, is a low granite massif that rises up between a vast plain in the north and the northern edge of the Tagus River estuary to a height of no more than 528 m (1732 ft). It is about 16 km (10 mi) long and 5 km (3 mi) wide at its widest point. The mountain undulates more or less east to west until it drops into the Atlantic Ocean at Cabo da Roca, the most western point of the entire Eurasian land mass.

Sintra. Built on the sloping northern side of the Serra, the small town of Sintra includes the historic Ville de Sintra (settled before Roman times) and the slightly more modern surrounding neighborhoods. Approximately 5,000 people live in the town today, a number that swells enormously during tourist season.

Sintra. One of the most popular tourist destinations in Portugal. An easy 45-minute train ride from Lisbon. And one of the most romantic places in the world.

Our "Powerful Places Guidebooks" usually focus on unusual and not-well-known sites. But *Powerful Places in Sintra* is an exception. That's because so many of Sintra's popular attractions are also powerful places. We invite you to explore Sintra not as casual tourists but as transformational travelers, open to deeply meaningful experiences. Admittedly, this can be complicated because Sintra's most celebrated attractions are visited by swarms of tourists. At busy times of day and year, it can be hard to get below the noisy, crowded, glitzy surface.

That's why we provide insider information and support. Each description of a site begins with a personal experience or observation, followed by background information, suggestions for getting the most out of your visit, and directions for how to get there. Unfamiliar words or terms are marked with an

* and defined in the glossary at the back. A ^ indicates an author is included in the bibliography.

In Part II, we provide suggestions that will help you have a deeper encounter with the seven most popular tourist attractions: the National Palace of Sintra, Quinta da Regaleira, the Park and Palace of Pena, the Moorish Castle, the Park and Palace of Monserrate, the Capuchos Convent, and Cabo da Roca. They are all part of the Sintra UNESCO World Heritage Site.

In Part III, we introduce you to a number of very special powerful places that are off the well-beaten path and are definitely worth exploring. These include megalithic sites, mysterious woodlands, ancient temples, and unusual Christian sanctuaries.

Powerful Places

We are often asked, "So, just what is a powerful place?" Based on our extensive experience, we define a powerful place as a place that feels—well, "different." A place where you feel unexpectedly energized, serene, a little spooked, filled with joy, covered with goosebumps, deeply grounded, terrified.... You get the idea.

Powerful places are found all over the world in nature: on mountaintops and inside caves, in forests and deserts, beside the ocean and on the banks of a river. Powerful places include places in nature linked to important events in human history: ancient

battlegrounds, the birthplace of a holy person, the appearance of a god or goddess.

In addition, powerful places are often intentionally constructed by Master Builders* using sacred geometry, astronomical alignments, and knowledge of earth energies. These sites include stone circles, dolmens, shrines, cathedrals, and temples. They are situated at those specific locations because of a combination of underground water channels and fault lines, telluric currents*, orientation to important celestial events (equinoxes, solstices, rising or setting of constellations), or to commemorate a theophany, the visible manifestation at that place of a god or goddess.

People experience the sacred through their unique cultural and religious lenses, and they name what they see accordingly. For example, Sintra Mountain is known as the Mountain of the Moon because of the more than 2,000-year-old written tradition that the goddess Diana wandered its mist-shrouded woodlands. Thousands of years before the Greeks and Romans arrived in Sintra, however, this goddess had a different name.

Since the 12th century, there have been at least four recorded apparitions on the mountain of a female deity. Because the people living in Sintra were now Christian, these manifestations were perceived as the Virgin Mary and Santa Eufemia. Three of these manifestations have been commemorated with sacred buildings at the locations where the goddess appeared: the original sanctuary of Our Lady of Pena, where the Palace of Pena now stands, the Church of Santa Eufemia, and the Sanctuary of Our Lady of Peninha. We will visit these places in this book.

A powerful place is built up in layers, like an onion.
- First, the geology of the land, including underground fault lines, water channels, magnetic anomalies, telluric currents, etc.
- Second, the ecology/environment/habitat/climate of the place.
- Third, the natural and human histories of the place. What natural events happened here (a volcano? an earthquake?)? What human events took place (a battle? an apparition?)? Who lived here and what did they do here? Was it a village, a burial place, a palace, a temple?
- Fourth, YOU, the person interacting with the place, bringing your own intentions and history to your experience.

How can you encounter a powerful place most fully? By centering, grounding, and being present to a site in whatever way works for you. Much of the time we humans operate "on automatic," hardly registering where we are or what we feel. Visiting a powerful place is an opportunity to be intentional and alert. In order to experience a powerful place, it is important to be present. Be aware of your surroundings and of subtle changes in yourself in response to the environment. Do you feel an unexpected change in temperature? A static charge on your skin? A faint fragrance wafting on the breeze?

Feeling the subtle energies in a place requires developing your sensitivity and intuition. It is a bit like tuning a radio dial to a particular frequency to get a clear signal and eliminate static. Although some people are naturally gifted in sensing these energies, others need to be taught. We didn't feel much at powerful places until we started studying with geomancers and dowsers.

Detailed instruction in sensing earth energies is outside the scope of this guidebook, but we give suggestions for how you can "attune" yourself to the powerful places we describe. Gary's book *The Dowsing Mind* is an excellent introduction to earth energies and provides practices for learning how to sense them.

We encourage you to listen carefully to your own inner guidance as you open yourself to what may be available to you at a powerful place on a particular day, at a particular time of day, with the unique disposition you bring to that moment. You must use your own judgment to determine what is good or not good for you. Trust your feelings. Leave a place if it doesn't feel right; stay if it feels good. And always, enjoy the mystery.

When approaching a human-constructed site:
• Remember that the site puts us in contact with the people who built it—not directly, but through the monuments themselves. People constructed them thousands of years ago. That's amazing. It's a kind of time travel.
• Explore the uniqueness of the site. Our ancestors expended a great deal of effort constructing it. Pay attention to the stones, the sacred geometry, and the underground energies that you may be able to sense.
• Enter into a relationship with the place, as if it were an animate, conscious being. Communicate with it; connect with it.
• Notice the Mystery: how everything *is*, but nobody knows what it *really* is.

Before entering a church, temple, or megalithic site—or an old-growth forest or sacred cave—pause a moment. Imagine that you are entering someone's home or place of worship: you wouldn't simply barge in without asking, and you would want to be polite. Ask permission from the spirits, the ancestors, or the guardians of the place*. If you sense a positive response before entering a sacred site, place your hand lightly on the standing stone or door frame to the right of the entryway. Attune yourself (come into energetic harmony) with the place. Then step over (not on) the threshold.

It's not always easy to be centered and present to a place, especially at popular tourist attractions. In addition, many powerful places and sacred sites are managed in such a way as to almost prevent you from having a meaningful experience. A chattering guide or audio earphones can take your attention away from being present to the place and keeps you in your head. Such diversions encourage you to look but not to see, to visit but not to experience.

This can be frustrating, so remember, and return to, the acronym **BLESSING.**

Breathe slowly and regularly, paying attention to your breath moving in and out. If you have a breathing practice, now is the time to do it.

Look and **L**isten within: what are you sensing internally? How do you feel?

Establish yourself in your location, perhaps by orienting to the seven directions (east, south, west, north, above, below, and the center within; or, before you, behind you, to your right, to your left, above, below, and in your heart).

Sense your surroundings, opening your five (or six) senses to what is around you.

State your **IN**tention to respect this place and to experience what is present.

Give gratitude for this opportunity.

With that preparation, let's begin our exploration of magical, mysterious Sintra!

A Very Brief History of Sintra

There's something about Sintra that has drawn people to live here for more than 7,000 years. Maybe it's the area's combination of natural beauty, powerful magnetic anomalies, abundant food and potable water sources, and proximity to the Colares River and the Atlantic Ocean. Paleolithic remains, ancient megalithic sites, Copper-Age vases, an exquisite 3,500-year-old gold collar, Iron-Age settlements, ruined Roman temples and villas, medieval fortifications, Renaissance monasteries, 19th-century estates, and expanding modern hamlets and towns all attest to this ongoing human habitation. Like the tides of the nearby ocean, Sintra's importance has ebbed and flowed but never entirely receded.

Sintra is like a palimpsest—a reused manuscript on which the previous message has been nearly effaced and written over. With careful attention, however, traces of the past can be reconstructed and even, sometimes, re-experienced.

For millennia, people have not only lived in Sintra, they have also worshipped here. Crescent-moon-shaped limestone artifacts and cave paintings attest to an ancient lunar cult* devoted to a powerful goddess of the moon and the hunt. This goddess was later known as Cynthia and

Artemis by the Greeks and as Diana during Roman occupation, which began around 150 BCE*.

The Roman temple at Alto da Vigia on the coast is proof of ongoing cultic practices devoted to the sun, moon, and the ocean: what better place for a temple than where the sun sinks into the sea and the moon sets behind the mountain? In the 2nd century CE*, a Roman writer referred to Sintra as "the Sacred Mountain," and the Greek geographer Ptolemy called it "the Mountain of the Moon," a clear reference to the Moon Goddess's ongoing importance in local memory, if not in practice.

Sintra Town and Around

Ancient megalith builders, early Iberians, Copper- and Iron-Age (Celtic) peoples, Phoenicians, Greeks, and Romans established themselves in the region. Over the millennia, some of the inhabitants stayed, some left, some merged into the communities of later settlers. In the 8th and 9th centuries, a new group arrived. Invading Moors from North Africa built an impressive fortress on the hilltop above Sintra. It was the perfect place to keep watch for invading Christian forces and protect nearby Lisbon and surrounding areas.

The Castelo dos Mouros/Moorish Castle (see p. 73) was built upon a Romanized proto-historic settlement—which was, in turn, built upon a much earlier one. Recent excavations have shown the same location was populated 7,000 years ago by Neolithic settlers, and

there is evidence of even earlier occupation on the mountain.

The Moorish Castle was captured without a struggle in 1147 by Christian forces under Dom Afonso Henriques (approx. 1106–1185), the first king of the country now called Portugal. He began transforming the former 10th- and 11th-century Muslim governor's palace in Sintra into a royal residence. As early as 1154, houses and lands in the area were donated by the king to Gualdim Pais, a master in the Order of the Knights Templar*, who was made responsible for running the town of Sintra and its environs.

By the 12th century, Christian churches and hermitages were established on the Sacred Mountain, often built over earlier sacred sites. This process of appropriation and syncretism has been going on for many millennia all over the world and has been practiced by many conquerors and many religions.

In those days, the area was already economically important and a source of abundant food and game. Not only Christians lived here; soon the town became the center of a significant Sephardic* community with a synagogue and its own neighborhood.

In 1281 King Dinis (1261–1325) promoted the further development of Sintra, including expanding the Moorish Castle and renovating the Palácio da Vila/Town Palace (see p. 40). What had begun as an Arab construction soon became a favorite abode of Portuguese royalty. But in 1348 came the Black Plague, and in 1356 an earthquake. The latter is not surprising, given that the Mountain of the Moon is an eruptive massif, indicative of underground seismic activity.

The Order of the Knights Templar*, founded in 1119, had been an important presence in Sintra since 1154, if not earlier (see Freddy Silva^ for an interesting perspective). Over the centuries, this order became extremely wealthy and powerful, which meant they also made powerful enemies. The French King Phillip IV (Phillip the Fair, 1268–1314), was deeply in their debt and jealous of their power. He wanted the Templars destroyed. In collusion with Pope Clement V, he ordered all the French Templars arrested on Friday the 13th of October, 1307. The Pope abolished the Order in 1312.

Dom Dinis refused to persecute the Portuguese Knights Templar, but in 1312 he complied with Pope

Clement's order and disbanded them. He then sent the ex-Templars to the south of Portugal. He rebranded them as the Military Order of Christ in 1319. This Order inherited the Templar personnel, lands, and assets. All that really changed was the name. Based on the extensive navigational knowledge of the Templars, the Military Order of Christ contributed to the first naval discoveries of the Portuguese. Infante Henrique the Navigator (1394–1460) led the Order for 20 years until the time of his death.

Beginning in the early 15th century, Dom João I (1357–1433) carried out extensive expansion works on the Town Palace, now known as the National Palace of Sintra (see p. 40). By the late 15th century, Portuguese kings and queens and their entourages spent more time in Sintra.

Dom Manuel I (1469–1521) made the National Palace of Sintra the most grandiose in Portugal, and the town itself naturally expanded. According to the king's chronicler, "because it is one of the places in Europe that is cooler, and cheerful for whichever King, Prince or Master to pass their time, because, in addition to its good airs, that cross its mountains, called by the older peoples the promontory of the moon, there is here much hunting of deer and other animals, and overall many and many good trout of many type, and

in which in all of Hispania there can be found, and many springs of water...." (King's chronicler).

Dom Manuel I ordered the construction of the Royal Monastery of Our Lady of Pena on the easternmost penha of Sintra Mountain. The monastery was later gifted to the Hieronymite Order, and in the 19th century, the building became the foundation of Pena Palace (see p. 85).

By 1527, Sintra was an impressive town with resident

knights and aristocrats. The abundance of hunting, the freshness of the climate in summer, and the need to escape the capital, Lisbon, during times of plague, all contributed to turning Sintra and its royal palace into a regular destination.

Renaissance-style palaces were constructed, including the Quinta de Penha Verde, built over an ancient Copper-Age settlement. In 1560, the Franciscan Convento dos Capuchos/Capuchos Convent* was founded by Álvaro de Castro, counselor to Dom Sebastião, on the mountainside, not far from the ancient megalithic site the Tholos do Monge (see p. 110 and p. 161).

Unfortunately, the heyday of Sintra ended with an abrupt and unwelcome political change. In 1581, the Hapsburg king of Spain, Philip II, grabbed control of Portugal and moved the seat of power to Vila Viçosa in the Alentejo. He and his court were not interested in more than an occasional visit to Sintra.

When the Portuguese monarchy was finally restored in 1640, Sintra had 4,000 residents. But its "disenchanted abandonment" did not improve. The restored Portuguese royalty found other places to visit for vacation, places more in keeping with their changing tastes and styles. Sintra slumped in importance and popularity.

On All Saints Day, 1755, Sintra, like much of this region, including Lisbon, experienced a devastating earthquake. People were killed and a large part of Sintra collapsed, including the palace, the Moorish Castle, and many churches. Many were soon rebuilt.

In the last quarter of the 18th century, Sintra began to recover its allure, thanks to touring pre-Romantic

writers and artists who left enthusiastic accounts of their visits to this enchanting place. Foreign travelers and Portuguese aristocrats rediscovered the fairytale magic of Sintra, as well as its pleasing climate. Impressive new buildings and country estates *(quintas)* were built or expanded upon.

In the 19th century, Romantic Sintra was well under development. The multicolored, turreted Pena Palace, the neo-Gothic Monserrate Palace, and the estates of Quinta de Regaleira and Quinta do Relógio were constructed, along with extensive and often fanciful gardens full of fake Romantic ruins and imported botanical species that thrive in the lush Sintra microclimate.

The development of the Sintra landscape reached its peak during the reign of Dom Fernando II of Saxe-Coburg and Gotha (1816–1885), who was heavily influenced by the Romanticism popular in his homeland. He acquired the Hieronymite Monastery and its lands. The property, like all others run by male monastic orders, had been nationalized by decree in 1834 and, as a result, abandoned. Dom Fernando II transformed the ruin into the Park and Palace of Pena (see p. 85), a multi-colored, multi-turreted fairytale castle, surrounded by extensive, romantic gardens filled with faux ruins, chapels, waterfalls, and so much more.

During the 1850s, the wealthy Englishman Sir Francis Cook turned an earlier, modest building and grounds on the Sintra hillside into the Parque e Palácio de Monserrate/Park and Palace of Monserrate (see p. 99), a dreamy edifice set in expansive gardens planted with rare specimens from around the world. Clearly, Sintra was at the apex of the architectural expression of Romanticism.

But there was more than just the construction of a few jewel-like palaces peering out from the forested Mountain of the Moon. There was also urban development. A train line was constructed to make Sintra more accessible from Lisbon. Houses were built in the new Estefânea neighborhood to house the railroad engineers, and the area around Sintra Ville (Historic Center of Sintra) began to expand. The railway was begun in 1854 or 1855 and inaugurated in 1887.

In 1892, the wealthy Brazilian-Portuguese António Augusto Carvalho Monteiro, the famous "Monteiro dos Milhões" (Millionaire Moneybags), purchased the Quinta da Regaleira estate on the outskirts of Sintra (see p. 53). He hired Italian set designer Luigi Manini to realize a complex construction project filled with esoteric/Masonic/Rosicrucian/Classical symbolism. Between 1904 and 1911, he oversaw the transformation of the quinta into a fascinating

collection of intriguing buildings, gardens, pavilions, lakes, man-made caves and tunnels, and initiatic wells.

By this time, Sintra was widely recognized as a popular summer resort by aristocrats and artists of all kinds, including writers, painters, and musicians. It also drew wealthy international visitors, attracted by the exuberant Romantic architecture.

In the early 20th century, economic development was promoted, emphasizing growth in agriculture, industry, and commerce. As a result, historic Sintra was radically and sometimes brutally transformed. Annexes to the National Palace of Sintra were torn down; roads were built or expanded, overlaying or destroying Roman roads, ancient settlements, and even part of the Church of the Misericordia. Numerous new buildings and factories were constructed, and the town expanded along the rail line.

At the same time, coastal Sintra became a growing center of summer tourism, resulting in the building of numerous new summer residences. By 1931, the Sintra Tourism Board was actively engaged in restructuring the town to make it even more attractive—and in safeguarding its patrimony.

Sintra has been protected since 1949 by the Sintra Urbanization Plan, designed to protect the town and its surroundings from uncontrolled urbanization. The plan also covers the nearby neighborhoods of São Pedro de Penaferrim (a small village on the hillside above Sintra), Estefânea, and Portela. This plan has maintained Sintra Ville—the Old Town—somewhat like it might have been in the 19th century, with its narrow alleys, small squares, and intriguing houses, all sheltered by the Serra de Sintra. New urban neighborhoods continued to develop in the areas around Sintra until the mid 1980s.

In 1995, Sintra and the Natural Park of Sintra-Cascais were declared a UNESCO World Heritage Cultural Landscape Site, a status that has undoubtedly helped promote its many attractions. Sintra is often ranked as the second or third most popular tourist site in Portugal, and Pena Palace often comes in first.

This explosion of popularity has radically changed the human presence in the Sintra region. Tens of

thousands of tourists take advantage of the frequent and rapid train connections from Lisbon to make a day-long visit to the romantic sites of Sintra. They alight from the train station and are greeted by tour guides, hop-on hop-off buses, motorized three-wheeled tuk-tuks, horse-drawn carriages, an articulated city train, and specially outfitted jeeps, all competing to take travelers on a quick tour of magical Sintra's most well-known attractions. Although these sites are well worth visiting, they are only a small part of what Sintra has to offer (see Part III, p. 131).

Sintra Municipality

The Municipality of Sintra encompasses much more than Sintra town and nearby attractions on the Mountain of the Moon. It has a population of 378,000 people scattered across 319 sq km (123 sq mi), many of them in small hamlets and towns. It is divided into 11 civil parishes (*freguesias*) for administrative purposes. Parts of the municipality are densely populated and urbanized, due to their proximity to Lisbon. It is one of the wealthiest and most expensive municipalities in Portugal. It is home to many expats who have settled along the so-called Portuguese Riviera, the affluent coastal region to the west of Lisbon that includes Cascais, Oeiras, and Sintra. If you visit Sintra town or drive any distance in the area, however, you will see more forested countryside than urban settlement.

Sintra Municipality contains three distinct regions: the mountain, the coast, and the plains. The climate near Cabo da Roca is considered semi-arid, but Sintra Mountain, located in the south of the municipality, is considered moderately humid and has a complex microclimate. The south side of the massif slopes more gently than the north, and the climate on that side is slightly warmer and dryer. The north side of the massif (where Sintra town is located) is cooler and wetter. It is prone to winds, mists, and fog, which can shift in an instant, veiling and unveiling the mountain peaks. The north side of the mountain gets more than twice the rainfall of the plains further to the north. The three regions have noticeable differences in climate, flora, and fauna.

Sintra Municipality encompasses the Sintra-Cascais Natural Park, a protected site since 1981 and declared a Natural Park in 1994. The 145 sq km (56 sq mi) Natural Park includes the Serra de Sintra coastal beaches and Cabo da Roca, the most western point in continental Europe. Opportunities abound for outdoor adventures of all sorts. The main tourist attractions are found on the Serra, within a short distance from Sintra town, but there is much more on offer. Hikers, bird watchers, and botanical seekers all find it worthwhile to explore the hillsides and the coast.

The Municipality contains a number of megalithic tholos*, *antas*, and dolmens*. One can also explore the remains of several Roman villas, including the one in the courtyard of the Archaeology Museum of São Miguel de Odrinhas, near São João das Lampas (see p. 170). The remains of an important Roman

temple and medieval Moorish *ribat** can be visited on a hillside above the beach at Praia das Maçãs (see p. 179) .

There are lovely beaches and charming seaside villages, including the stunning Azenhas do Mar, perched on a cliff overlooking the Atlantic. There are 18th-century palaces and parks (Queluz National Palace and Seteais Palace, the latter turned into a 5-star Tivoli Hotel in 1954) within easy reach. If you are interested in wine tasting, the nearby town of Colares is famous for its DOC* wine production, which escaped the phylloxera plague that decimated many European vineyards in the early 20th century. The Colares grapevines are planted directly on sand, and the phylloxera aphids cannot live in that environment.

You could spend weeks, months—a lifetime—exploring the powerful places in magical Sintra town, the Mountain of the Moon, and the surrounding municipality. But most travelers don't have that much time, so we have included only the most important sites in this guidebook, although we mention others.

Sintra Mountain/The Mountain of the Moon

The geology of Sintra may be part of what has drawn people to it for much longer than 7,000 years.

Geology

The Serra de Sintra/Sintra Massif/Sintra Mountain/Mountain of the Moon was formed 90–95 million years ago, when silica-rich magma (molten rock) from the center of the earth invaded the layers of much older sedimentary rock (limestone and sandstone) and hardened into granite. This intrusion pushed the sedimentary stone higher, cracking and distorting it. Cracking resulted in what are called "faults," and the distortion resulted in "folding."

The heat and pressure of the intrusion also changed the structure of some of the sedimentary rock, forming various types of metamorphic stone. The resulting mixture of sedimentary rock, granite, and metamorphic rock was harder than the surrounding limestone and sandstone. Over eons, the landmass

was eroded by wind, rain, and the constant pounding of the Atlantic Ocean. What was left behind is what we call Sintra Mountain: a mostly granite massif rising out of the surrounding plains.

The low, forest-covered mountain, no higher than 529 m (1,736 ft), has a number of hilltop peaks, or *penhas*. Deep valleys separate many of them. At its widest point, Sintra Mountain is 5 km (3 mi) wide. The massif undulates like a lumbering dragon east to west for 16 km (10 mi) until it drops into the ocean at Cabo da Roca, the most western point in the Eurasian land mass (see p. 122).

Hidden beneath the waves at the Cabo is an underwater extension of Sintra Mountain, which for centuries has been a hazard for ships. The region off the coast of the Cabo is littered with ancient shipwrecks. A lighthouse was erected in 1772 at Cabo da Roca to warn ships to steer clear of the area.

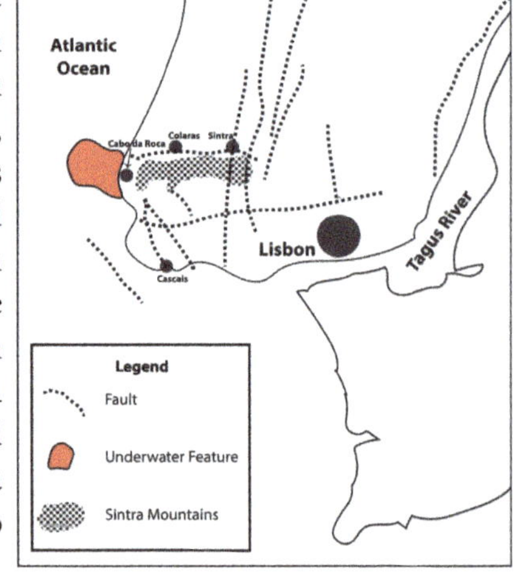

Given the topography of the mountain, going from one location to another can feel confusing. Places may look quite close to each other from a distance, but it takes a long time to travel between them. Some sites seem quite distant but are actually on neighboring hilltops. For example, although the Palace of Pena and the Castle of the Moors seem quite separate, it is only a short distance between the main entrances to the two attractions if you approach by road. However, if you follow the hiking trail up from Sintra to the Castle, you will be on a very different hillside than the Palace.

As you view the mountain from different perspectives, the relationship of the palaces and castles perched on its top and sides changes. Perhaps that also adds to the mysterious allure of Sintra.

Geological Anomalies

The mountain is a complex geological mixture of different kinds of stone, faults, and folds. As a result of its turbulent history, there are many internal tensions and pressures. One result of this is that Sintra Mountain is subject to variations in perceived magnetic north, a phenomenon called a magnetic anomaly. People report all kinds of strange interferences with compasses, batteries, watches, and other electronic devices. In addition, a large mass of iron hidden within part of the mountain appears to explain why a stopped car is reported to roll uphill at a particular location on the road that winds its way around the massif.

Much of the massif consists almost entirely of various types of granite. Granite is a mixture of quartz, feldspar, mica, and several other igneous rocks, locked together in a matrix of various sizes of crystals. If granite forms deep under the earth and

cools very slowly, the crystals become quite large and are clearly visible. If the molten rock forms nearer the surface, it hardens before the crystals have time to grow, the texture is much finer, and it is difficult to see the individual components. If feldspar is the predominant component of the stone, it has a pink to red/orange color. If darker igneous rock, such as hornblende, predominates, the color is grey to nearly black. If the predominant mineral is quartz, which is clear or lighter in color, the granite may be quite light in color. All kinds of granite are visible in the Sintra Mountain.

Granite is a very special kind of rock. It is extremely hard and strong, and it resists breaking and eroding. The hilltops of Sintra Mountain have large deposits of granite, visible in huge boulders and massive cliffs. Granite is mildly radioactive, and that may have some effect on those who live near large deposits. If you are sensitive to subtle energies, you may be able to sense the power of granite in your body. The trail up to the Moorish Castle (see p. 73), the area just below Peninha (see p. 132), Cabo da Roca (see p. 122), and the Pedras Irmãs (Sisters Stones) (see p. 133) are good places to come into intimate contact with large amounts of granite. Use the suggestions we give in the Introduction (see pp. 9–10) for visiting a powerful place and see what you feel.

Granite on Sintra Mountain contains large quantities of quartz. Quartz (silica dioxide) is extremely resistant to weathering and dissolution by chemicals. It is used in watches and clocks because it vibrates at a precise frequency. When compressed, quartz produces electricity, an effect called piezoelectricity—in other words, it can give off a measurable charge. These properties may account for some of the effects produced by large deposits of granite.

A mixture of environments, a long history of human habitation, powerful geological formations—all contribute to the mystique of Sintra.

Travel Tips

Sintra is a very popular day trip from Lisbon, although it's much better to allow three or four days to experience this magical place and its surroundings.

When to Go

Sintra can get very busy in summer, so off-season is a great time to visit. Even in winter, it isn't too cold, though it's wise to check your weather app. It's also advisable to get started early in the day (some attractions open at 9:30 in summer, 10:00 in winter) and to avoid weekends, especially at Pena Palace and Quinta da Regaleira. Although you can rush through three or four of the major sites in a single day, several of the palaces have elaborate gardens and extensive parks that take time to explore.

Transportation

Trains and buses run frequently between Sintra and Lisbon, Estoril, and Cascais. (Comboios de Portugal Trains, QR code to the left.) The buses stop, among other places, in front of the train station. You can also drive to Sintra, but driving your own car to the popular attractions or within Sintra town is not recommended. Many streets are one way, and you can end up heading out of town before you know it. There is often nowhere to park and driving your own car to nearby tourist sites significantly adds to the traffic congestion. In addition, road access to the Moorish Castle and the

Park and Palace of Pena is limited to residents and authorized tourist vehicles like buses, Bolt, and Uber.

Sintra town is built on the sloping side of the Serra de Sintra, a low granite massif. The National Palace in Old Town Sintra is 900 m (.56 mi) from the train station, and Quinta da Regaleira is another 3/4 km (1/2 mi) from the National Palace. Pena Palace, Monserrate Palace, the Capuchos Convent*, and the Moorish Castle are located higher up or on top of the mountain. They can be reached by public transport (see below) or, if you are a good hiker, by road or numerous trails. If you choose to walk to them, wear good walking shoes and carry a daypack with a water bottle and snacks.

We suggest you download one or two walking apps, such as AllTrails, Walkbox, WalkSintra, or WalkMe. The Visit Sintra website provides details for walking the PR (short route) trails: https://visitsintra.travel/en/discover/active-sintra/land-sports/hiking/

Hiking Trails in Sintra

There are numerous transport options for getting to the most popular attractions. The most economical are the two bus lines, Scotturb and CitySightseeing. Scotturb tourist bus 434 will take you up the very steep hillside to the Moorish Castle and Pena Palace,

Scotturb Mobile App

among other sites. Scotturb tourist bus 435 will take you to Quinta da Regaleira, Seteais Palace, and Monserrate Palace and Park. You can hop-on and hop-off of either bus.

City Sight-seeing Bus

Bright red hop-on hop-off CitySightseeing buses are more expensive but also have fewer passengers and often are double-decker and open on top. There are two routes. The Blue Route is more local; the Red Route includes coastal towns and Cabo da Roca.

Tuk-tuks (motorized three-wheeler vehicles) and their enthusiastic, often colorfully dressed drivers will take you where you want to go, but at a cost. There are also jeep tours, organized bus tours, taxis, an articulated city train, and horse-drawn carriages. Bolt and Uber are also popular. Or you can rent an e-bike. Always follow standard safety procedures when using ride-call apps. Be sure the driver takes

you to the front ticket office of the main attractions and not the back entrance. (We once got dropped off at the beginning of a popular hiking trail up the mountain to the Moorish Castle, a hike we were not prepared to undertake.)

It is a mostly level, 15-minute stroll from the train station to the Historic Center (Sintra Ville/Historic Center) and the National Palace of Sintra. The National Palace (not to be confused with Pena Palace) is recognizable from a distance by its two large white cone-shaped chimneys (see p. 40).

If you arrive by train and want to start your explorations in Sintra Ville, walk downhill from the station and turn left on the Volta da Duche, a U-shaped road lined with sculptures and, often, with vendors selling artisanal crafts of all sorts. Along the way you will pass the main entrance to the delightful Parque de Liberdade (well worth strolling through) and the charming 20th-century Fonte Mourisca, a tile-lined, Arabesque water fountain.

Once your reach the Historic Center and the National Palace of Sintra, you will find numerous hotels, guest houses, restaurants, cafes, and gift shops, some specializing in Port tastings and craft beers. If you want to fortify yourself before continuing your explorations, indulge in one of several classic Portuguese sweets: the custard tart called pastel de nata—be sure to sprinkle cinnamon on top—or the Sintra specialties queijadas (a fresh-cheese mini-tart wrapped in crisp pie pastry) and travesseiros (log-shaped, almond-cream-filled puff pastries dusted with powdered sugar).

It is another 3/4 km (1/2 mile), a 10-minute stroll, from the National Palace of Sintra in the Historic Center to

Quinta da Regaleira. You can also walk to Pena Palace and the Moorish Castle, which are relatively close to each other, but the walk is unrelentingly uphill and takes time. Monserrate Palace, the Capuchos Convent, and Cabo da Roca require motorized transport.

Tickets

You can buy individual or combined tickets online or at the main attractions. If you buy online, you can schedule your ticket time in advance and skip the long lines when you arrive. The discount for combined purchase is minimal. Go to https://www.parquesdesintra.pt/en/ for the latest information on opening hours, scheduling tickets, etc. You can also call (+351) 219 237 300 for assistance in English.

Parques de Sintra Website

You can purchase and download audiovisual guides to play on your smartphone. There is a discount if you buy them all at once. There are also guided tours on offer at different sites, some of which must be booked in advance.

The Parques de Sintra website does not sell tickets for Quinta da Regaleira. The Quinta is administered by Cultursintra Foundation, a part of the Sintra Town Hall, and requires a separate ticket. For more information, go to http://www.regaleira.pt/en/ Booking a group tour is done by going to https://regaleira.byblueticket.pt; an online calendar lists availability

Quinta da Regaleira Website

of tours in different languages. You will need to plan in advance because there is limited availability, especially for English-language tours. Audio guides can be rented at the ticket office. You can also call (+351) 219 106 650 for assistance in English.

In general, it is always best to check online for the latest information and discounts and, perhaps, to schedule your visit in advance, especially if you want an onsite tour in English. During tourist season, ticket lines at the main attractions can be very long.

Some useful contacts:
Sintra Tourism Office
Praça República 23, 2710-616 Sintra
Sintra 2710-616 PT
Phone: (+351) 219 231 157
Website: http://www.sintraromantica.net/
Parques de Sintra - Monte da Lua, S.A.
Phone: (+351) 219 237 300
Email: info@parquesdesintra.pt
Website: http://www.parquesdesintra.pt/en/
Quinta da Regaleira
Reservations: reservas@cultursintra.pt
Information: (+351) 219 106 650 or
geral@cultursintra.pt
Address: Quinta da Regaleira, 9, 2710-567 Sintra, Portugal | GPS 38°47'45.15"N - 9°23'50.21"O
Website: http://www.regaleira.pt/en/

Some Quirks We Have Noticed

Sometimes when you search for an address in Sintra on Google, you will see "Sintra (Santa Maria e São Miguel, e São Martinho, e São Pedro de Penaferrim)." These names in parentheses refer to the long-standing administrative division of the town into four parishes.

The gift shops at the main attractions may or may not keep the same schedule as the attraction itself. Often, the gift shops close for an hour or more during lunchtime or early afternoon. Guidebooks for each attraction are available only at the associated gift shop. If visiting the gift shop is important to you, check at the entrance to the attraction to find out when the gift shop is open and closed.

Ticket offices also are sometimes closed, but there are usually automated ticket vending machines available. It is most advisable to check online at https://www.parquesdesintra.pt/en/ or http://www.regaleira.pt/en/ before going anywhere, and to be aware that sometimes websites are not always updated regularly.

The Tourist Office in Sintra Ville (the Historic Center of Sintra) (Praça da República, 23; telephone (+351) 219 231 157) has an interactive exhibit called "Myths and Legends of Sintra." Tickets are inexpensive and can be purchased at the entrance. Allow about an hour for the experience. The gift shop sells souvenirs and a few guidebooks but does not have guidebooks for individual attractions.

Do not expect bus schedules to be kept to the minute or even 10 minutes. Given the fluctuating number of tourists, buses may arrive earlier, later, or skip a stop entirely. Traffic flow has been rerouted in recent years, but there can still be congestion on the narrow mountain roads leading to the main attractions on the Mountain of the Moon.

A surprising number of people, especially professionals and hospitality providers, speak English. Many tourist attractions include English translations of Portuguese-language information, and there are English-language options when you call them for information. That said, you will also encounter people—including Bolt and Uber drivers—who do not speak English.

It is very helpful to have a translation app on your smartphone so you can either play the Portuguese translation aloud or show it to someone. Obviously, this doesn't work as well during a phone call. Fortunately, most Portuguese are friendly and helpful if you make an effort to communicate. Just so you know, the smartphone translation apps all appear to use Brazilian Portuguese, which has a different accent and some different vocabulary from European Portuguese.

In large towns, many establishments accept foreign credit cards (rarely Amex) for payment. However, sometimes a store will only accept a Portuguese credit/debit card or cash. The smaller the town and the smaller the establishment, the more likely you will need to pay with cash. Be sure you know your credit card code in numbers, not letters.

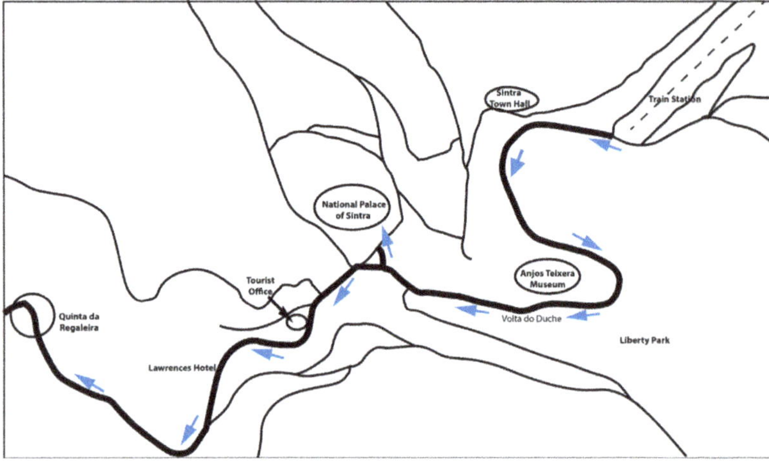

Walking route from the Sintra train station to the National Palace of Sintra and Quinta da Regaleira

Part II—The Top Attractions

We begin our exploration of Sintra with the main tourist attractions, organized in terms of their proximity to Sintra town: the National Palace of Sintra, Quinta da Regaleira, the Park and Palace of Pena, the Moorish Castle, the Park and Palace of Monserrate, the Capuchos Convent, and Cabo da Roca. Tickets are required for all but Cabo.

Palácio Nacional de Sintra/ The National Palace of Sintra

"It's a place of power—political power that is. If you like palaces it's a good one—not too big, not too small, with interesting and varied architecture, including numerous design styles and multi-leveled gardens. The well-placed windows provide excellent views of the Moorish Castle on the hillside and the twisting spires of nearby Quinta da Regaleira. Every room is different. Geometric-patterned and blue-and-white narrative azulejos (tiles), a rare Mudejar* wood-coffered ceiling, a room topped with an elaborately decorated heraldic cupola, a 17th-century, silver 'bed of state'—all make the visit worthwhile." —Elyn*

Background

The National Palace of Sintra is not our usual kind of powerful place—it doesn't give us chills or shivers; it doesn't fill us with awe. However, it is definitely a place of power: its occupation spans 800 years, nearly the entire history of the nation we call Portugal. This makes it the oldest national palace in Portugal, and nearly every Portuguese king and queen spent time here. The palace's development and use over the centuries enables us to see the how architecture reflects history and political power.

The palace's unmistakable white Gothic exterior, marked by two very large (33 m tall) conical chimneys, sometimes described as upside-down champagne flutes, rises above the historic center of Sintra. What we see today is a conglomeration of remodeling and additions that transformed the small castle of the Moorish governor of the region into a Renaissance palace fit for Portuguese monarchs.

The Moors from North Africa invaded the Iberian Peninsula in 711 and what we now call Portugal in 756. Portugal remained part of Al-Andalus* for more than 300 years. The National Palace was built upon the (still-undiscovered) remains of the Moorish governor's palace that probably originated in the 10th century, in what was known as The Olive Grounds. An 11th-century Andalusian Arab geographer wrote about Sintra and its two castles, one presumably the Moorish castle on the hill and the other the residence of the Moorish governor in the town itself.

During the Christian Reconquest* of Iberia, known as the Reconquista, Dom Alfonso Henriques (approx. 1106– 1185) conquered the Moors in Sintra in 1147. Dom Afonso Henriques became the first king of the nation we now call Portugal, but which was then a smaller territory known as Portucale. (The southern part of Portugal, the Algarve, continued under Moorish rule until 1249.)

The earliest written record of the Christian palace dates to 1281, during the reign of Dom Dinis (1261–1325). Dom Dinis added the Palantine (Royal) Chapel and lowered the tax burdens of the free Moors living in nearby Colares in exchange for their conservation work on the palace. At that time, the palace was notably smaller.

In 1287, Dom Dinis gifted the palace and the town of Sintra to his wife, Dona Isabel of Aragon, "the Holy Queen." Within a century, this practice of gifting the palace and town to the reigning queen had become routine, and the queens of Portugal became overseers of the vast amount of income and tax revenues generated by the town and its properties. The palace became known as the Queens House, and the income was used to support the queen's courtly expenses.

Dom João I (1357–1433) and Dona Filipa de Lencastre expanded the palace, constructed chambers around the central patio, added the Swan Room and adjoining rooms, and built the very large kitchen with its two iconic and ostentatious chimneys. By constructing such an opulent dwelling, the king demonstrated

his status as the powerful founder of the new Avis dynasty.

Dom João I also began Portuguese imperialism with the capture of the North African city of Ceuta in 1415. His son Henrique the Navigator commissioned expeditions to the west coast of Africa, whereupon Portuguese maritime expansion—the so-called Age of Discovery—began in earnest.

During the 15th century, the kings and queens of Portugal and their entourages began spending more time in Sintra, enjoying the abundant game, both large (wild boar and deer) and small (hare and partridge) that thrived in the lush hillsides of the Serra. Nearby Lisbon had developed into the bureaucratic center

of the kingdom, and Sintra was quite close, easy to access, and enjoyed a more favorable summer climate.

Dom Manuel I (1469–1521) developed the palace further, including the East Wing, complete with added Manueline* features and Mudejar* elements

such as the Hispano-Moresque tiling. He also added the impressive Coat of Arms Room with its elaborate cupola, featuring the coats of arms of the king, his children, and 72 noble households. He turned the palace into the most grandiose in Portugal, using the wealth (and gold) brought back from successful maritime ventures he promoted, including Vasco de Gama's voyage to India in 1498.

The claiming of Brazil as a Portuguese colony in 1500 catapulted Portugal into enormous wealth and international power. The extensive Manueline ornamentation in the National Palace, full of maritime references, including large twisted ropes, nautical images, and oceanic and botanical symbols, is a visual representation of Portugal's Age of Discovery.

Dom João III (1502–1557) expanded the palace, connecting the main chambers to the south with the northeastern wing. The Renaissance palace that we see today is much like it has been since João III's renovations in the mid-16th century.

The palace was one of the favorite places of Dom Sebastião (1554–1578), whose bedroom can still be seen. Unfortunately, Dom Sebastião ended the Age of Discovery with a disastrous expedition to Morocco in 1578. He died there without an heir, and his ghost is said to wander at night through the fog-shrouded forests on Sintra Mountain. But that's another story....

In 1580, Philip II of Spain claimed the right through inheritance to the Portuguese throne, and in 1581, Portugal came under unwelcome Spanish control. In 1640, Lisbon revolted, and the Duke of Bragança was named Dom João IV. Spain retaliated, and the resulting War of Restoration continued until 1668, at which time Portugal won Spanish recognition of its independence.

During the Spanish reign, Sintra and its National Palace were neglected. Philip II visited Sintra and

spent a night in the palace, which he described as old but with very good rooms. The palace ceased to be a popular dwelling place for the monarchy and the court.

Dom Afonso VI (1643–1683), the second king of Portugal of the House of Bragança, saw the end of the Restoration War. However, he was physically and mentally weak, and in 1674, his brother Pedro conspired to have him imprisoned until his death in the National Palace of Sintra. After that, the long decline of the palace continued, although Dom Pedro II (1648–1706) conducted major restoration work. The palace, however, was only lived in sporadically after that.

In 1755, the major earthquake that leveled parts of Lisbon and Sintra also impacted the National Palace. Major reconstruction was undertaken rapidly, thanks to the enormous amount of gold plundered from Brazil.

Dona Maria I (1734–1816) had work carried out on the gardens and palace beginning in 1787. It was during this period that William Beckford, a very wealthy and eccentric Englishman, became enchanted with Sintra. He was part of a stream of privileged European travelers, artists, and writers who took part in a pre-Romantic-era Grand Tour. They fell in love with Sintra and extolled its magical and mysterious qualities.

In 1807, Napoleon invaded Portugal and the Royal Family fled to Brazil. Portugal was soon embroiled in the Peninsular War (1808–1814). Although Napoleon was defeated, the Royal Family did not return to Portugal and the National Palace of Sintra until 1821, after the Liberal Revolution of 1820.

In 1822, a constitutional monarchy was established in Portugal. The National Palace was adapted to be more fitting for domestic life since it was no longer the central seat of political power.

Dom Fernando II (1816–1885) was a German prince of the House of Saxe-Coburg and Gotha-Koháry; he married Dona Maria II of Portugal. He was king of Portugal from the birth of their first son in 1837 to her death in 1853. The monarchs lived in Palácio das Necessidades in Lisbon.

Dom Fernando II was widely read, very cultured and artistic, and steeped in Romanticism. In 1838, he acquired the former Hieronymite monastery of Our Lady of Pena on the hill above Sintra. He transformed it into the eclectic Romantic fantasy known as the Park and Palace of Pena (see p. 85). After Maria II's death, Dom Fernando II chose to live in Pena Palace.

Dona Maria Pia, the widow of Dom Luís (1839–1889), spent summers and her last days in Portugal in the palace, before departing into exile in October 1910. The revolution of 1910 ended the monarchy and the role of the palace as a royal residence. It was declared a National Monument in 1910.

During the late 1930s, renovations were undertaken under dictator António de Oliveira Salazar's *Estado Novo* regime (1933–1975) to turn the National Palace into a propaganda vehicle extoling Portugal's grand past. After extensive restoration and rearrangement of the rooms, the palace opened its doors to the public in the late 1930s as a kind of museum to a glorified past.

In 1974, The Carnation Revolution* peacefully eradicated dictatorial power, and Portugal began becoming the democratic republic that it is today. The revolution also ended the Portuguese colonial empire, which had been the source of so much wealth as well as so much conflict.

In 1995, the National Palace became part of the UNESCO World Heritage Cultural Landscape Site of Sintra.

What to Explore

As a result of more than 800 years of occupation and renovation, the National Palace is an amalgam of styles, including Mudejar*, Gothic*, Manueline*, and Renaissance*. We will mention just a few. The audiovisual guide (available for rent at the ticket office) and information plaques in each room provide detailed information.

Don't miss the Magpie Room, where the ceiling is covered with 136 painted magpies. Banners hang from their beaks that read "por bem" ("for good") and roses hang from their claws. It is said that the ceiling is a subtle reference to Dona Filipa seeing Dom

João I present a flower to a lady of the court. Caught in the act, he apologized and said that his action was "por bem"—"well intentioned." The queen forgave him, but the ladies of the court spread the story. In revenge, the king immortalized the gossiping ladies as garrulous magpies. The walls are covered with stunning star-motif Hispano-Moresque tiles from the early 16th century.

Don't miss the Sala dos Brasões, the splendid 16th-century Coats of Arms room. When you enter the room through the magnificent Manueline doorway, notice the monograms carved in the stone: these are the marks of the master masons. The elaborately paneled octagonal dome displays the coats of arms of Dom Manuel I, his eight children, and 72 most valued aristocratic families. Below the ornate shields are Delft-like tiled pictorial panels created from 1710–1715.

The former banqueting hall is the Room of the Swans (*Cisnes*). The ceiling is divided into 27 octagonal coffered sections decorated with swans, each wearing a golden collar. The white swans stand for purity and fidelity.

The Palantine (Royal) Chapel can be looked down upon from the upper level of the palace. This provides an excellent view of the rare Mudejar* coffered wood ceiling. The chapel is oriented not to the east, as is

usual, but in the direction of Mecca. Dom Dinis founded the chapel in the early 14th century; Dom Afonso V added the high altar (now lost) in the second half of the 15th century. The ceiling is exceptional, using the *alfarge* technique of geometric stellate or radial patterns carved in wood. This was popular in the Iberian Peninsula in the 15th and 16th centuries. The Mudejar* ceiling in Sintra is reported to be the oldest that survives. The Mudejar floor is also noteworthy, created from ceramic tiles in many colors and shapes that form geometric patterns.

As you walk through the palace, you will reach the charming Arab Room with geometric tiles and its central fountain. The fountains and tiles were created during the reign of Dom Manuel I but have become a symbol of the Moorish legacy.

Soon you will come to the "Room with a 17th-century State Bed." The central feature is an impressive black wood silver-adorned canopied bed. Although not original to the palace, sumptuous beds of this kind were placed in state rooms in Portuguese royal palaces and noble residences. They were opulently covered in rich cloths and were recognized as symbols of wealth and prestige. Referred to since the Middle Ages as "the State Bed," the bed was less intended for sleep and more intended to demonstrate power. Deeply

symbolic, it was associated with important rites of passage, including marriage, birth, and death.

There are many other rooms worthy of note, including the Room of the Mermaids and the Chinese or Pagoda Room. In all, there are more than 18 rooms to visit, three courtyards, and four charming gardens. The gardens can be visited without charge. The gardens are laid out in terraces to the west of the palace. The gardens (and many of the windows of the palace) offer exceptional views of the hills, the Moorish Castle,

the historic town center, and the nearby Quinta da Regaleira. Many of the rooms have interesting furnishings as well. Allow a few hours to explore the palace, especially if you take time to read the displays and listen to the audio recording.

Getting There/Other Information

The National Palace of Sintra is in the Historic Center, an easy 1 km (5/8 mi) walk from the train station. Tickets and an extensive downloadable audiovisual guide can be purchased at the ticket office, accessed by climbing the main staircase in front of the palace. You can also buy combined tickets and audiovisual guides for other tourist attractions at this ticket office at a discount.

There's a gift shop upstairs and a cafeteria accessible through the palace, via the narrow staircase to the far left that leads to the gardens, or via the steep narrow staircase to the left of the main entrance. If you want to visit the gift shop, make sure you check its opening hours; it may be closed during lunchtime. The cafeteria was closed in 2021 because of COVID and may not be open.

https://www.parquesdesintra.pt/en/parks-monuments/national-palace-of-sintra/

Quinta da Regaleira

"It seems both larger and smaller than it really is, an elaborate stage set built into and out of the natural landscape. As you follow the winding paths through the grounds of the estate, reality blurs with illusion, and soon you have crossed into the Imaginal Realm, a place where nothing is what it seems. That towering tree trunk? A disguised incinerator chimney. That ancient, moss-covered dolmen? An artfully arranged, modern pile of boulders. Wander through the park as a tourist, or enter into an initiatic journey. The choice is yours." —Elyn

Background

The Regaleira Estate includes a palace and chapel, grottoes, tunnels, towers, a ziggurat, elaborate fountains, an initiatic well, lakes, a plethora of statuary, and extensive gardens. It may seem at first like a miniature Euro-Disneyland, built to entertain, but it is, in fact, a carefully orchestrated symbolic landscape. It was constructed not as a tourist attraction but for the owner's personal use, a manifestation of his deeply held philosophical beliefs.

The Quinta is the brainchild of "Moneybags Millionaire" António Augusto Carvalho Monteiro (1848–1920), a wealthy Brazilian-Portuguese businessman, lawyer, entomologist, book collector, and monarchist. He purchased the estate in 1892 from Ermelinda Allen Monteiro de Almeida, the Viscountess of Regaleira, and he transformed it into what it is today.

There had been many other owners before those two, however, including the Order of the Knights Templar* in the 12th century. Little is known of what happened to the estate during the next few centuries, but it is possible it belonged to the Franciscan Order in the 15th–16th centuries. In 1697, it was purchased by José Manuel Lopes Leite.

In 1715, Guimarães de Castro acquired the land, which was then known as Quinta da Torre, after a tower built in the grounds. According to the esoteric writer Vitor Manuel Adrião^, during this time the property became part of the Via Sacra* or Caminho das Cruzes* that led from the Royal Palace of Sintra (see p. 40) to the Royal Monastery of Nossa Senhora da Pena (see p. 85). Perhaps this pilgrimage route continued to resonate in the Quinta and influenced Carvalho Monteiro nearly two centuries later to transform the estate into an initiatic journey.

In 1800, the Quinta was purchased by João António Lopes Fernandes and in 1830 by Manuel Bernardo Fernandes, who may have been a Freemason. In 1840 the Quinta was purchased by the Viscountess of Regaleira, and the Quinta da Torre became the Quinta da Regaleira.

Carvalho Monteiro bought the property in 1892 and hired the Italian architect and operatic set designer Luigi Manini to create an environment based on esoteric, Christian, and Classical symbolism. Between 1904 and 1910, Manini transformed the four-hectare estate into an enigmatic collection of buildings, fountains, and monuments in numerous architectural styles, including Romanesque*, Gothic*, Renaissance*, and Manueline*, scattered around the carefully constructed Romantic gardens.

> "The Romantic style…is a style in which everything is designed down to the last detail and constructed in such a way as to appear natural, whilst at the same time conveying a suggestion of the supernatural, as if man could play a hand in the divine gift of recreating and embellishing nature." (Quinta audioguide)

Carvalho Monteiro died in 1920, and in 1942, the estate was sold to Waldemar d'Orey, who used it as a summer home and had parts of the property restored more to his taste. In 1987, the estate was sold to the Japanese Aoki Corporation, which closed the property to the public. In 1997, the Sintra Town Council acquired it, and, after extensive restoration efforts, the Quinta was opened to the public in 1998. It is part of the Sintra UNESCO World Heritage Site.

What to Explore

Quinta da Regaleira is more than a collection of intriguing buildings set in a beautiful park. It is a carefully calibrated set design intended to lead the participant up, down, around, and through a powerful transformation experience. At least that's what many researchers believe, although there is no written evidence that it was ever used this way. Of course, such initiatic practices would have been secret, so lack of written evidence does not negate the possibility. According to José Manuel Anes^, the Quinta is an ecumenical place " where Paganism and Christianity coexist" along with several "references to literary and initiatory traditions."

The numerous buildings, towers, wells, galleries, and fountains are (literally) covered with symbols associated with alchemy, hermeticism, Freemasonry, the Knights Templar*, the Grail quest, and the Rosicrucians. Within the elaborate décor of the Quinta are hidden (and not so hidden) references to Portuguese epic poetry, Greco-Latin classical authors, Dante, and the coming of a New Age of the World. Remember: the Quinta was intentionally designed to express a set of philosophical beliefs. Unlike Disneyland, the plethora of visual input is not merely decorative.

Allow plenty of time for your visit and, if possible, start early in the morning on a weekday, when the estate is less crowded. Although it's possible to rush through the gardens to descend into the famous Poço Iniciático/Initiatic Well, it is much better to walk contemplatively along the meandering footpaths, listening to the rented audio guide, and soaking in the rich complexity of the place. We could write a book about the Quinta, but instead we will highlight four of the many constructions and then explore in depth the Initiatic Well.

Palácio/Palace

The Palace of Regaleira is where Monteiro and his family lived. It has five floors, including a basement; the main floor is open for visitors. The ornate sculpture-covered exterior includes gargoyles, animals, a lizard holding the Philosopher's Egg, a dragon representing telluric currents*, a Green Man* with vines coming out of its mouth, effigies, cameos of famous people, sculptures of Monteiro's family, an octagonal

tower, and numerous soaring pinnacles. The interior, however, is surprisingly domestic in scale. The Billiard or Monarch's Room has a noteworthy ceiling featuring the Portuguese monarchs from Dom Afonso Henriques to João V. Because Monteiro was a proud monarchist and Portuguese nationalist, he omitted the Spanish kings who ruled Portugal between 1580–1640.

Capela/ Chapel

The beautifully proportioned neo-Manueline Roman Catholic chapel is a homage to Mary, with numerous nods to the Masons, hermetic and alchemical symbolism, the Knights Templar*, and the Portuguese Military Order of Christ*, into which the Templars morphed (see p. 14). It has been called the most densely symbolic building in the Quinta.

Richly worked filigree, elaborate pinnacles, and numerous sculptures adorn the chapel's white façade. It is laden with symbolism just waiting to be interpreted—or misinterpreted. Are the numerous carvings and stained-glass windows expressing traditional Catholic iconography, or do they hint at hidden esoteric meanings? The challenge is to discern what

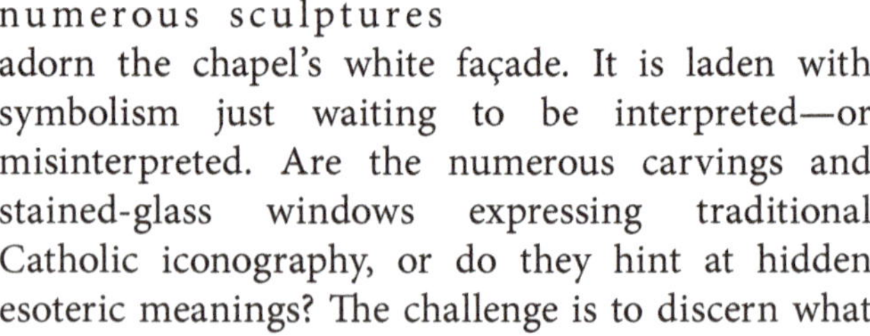

was intended by the creators of the building and what is imposed by contemporary visitors, who interpret through the lens of their own belief systems.

For example, the cross of the Order of Christ is visible on the rooftop. Is that meant to evoke the Knights Templar and their perhaps heretical beliefs? The exterior door to the sacristy has numerous sculptures. Is the Morning Star carved on the doorframe a reference to the Virgin Mary or to an ancient goddess, either Isis or Venus? Is the cup with a wafer a reference to Communion or a hint about the Holy Grail? Is the lamb a symbol of Christ or a veiled reference to the Knights Templar? Is the dove the Holy Spirit or the symbol of the Order of Sion? That's the nature of esoteric art: it can be interpreted many ways.

One sculpture apparently has an undeniable alchemical reference. Located on the outside wall near the sacristy door, the Athanor is a castle with twin towers with an arched grid between; below is a face with gaping mouth and flaming hair. This is an alchemical symbol representing the furnace (athanor) used by the Adept in the Great Work, and the open mouth symbolizes the prophetic capacity given by the Philosopher's stone. Or maybe (according to Freddy Silva^), it represents the castle of Mary Magdalene and Martha (the Templars may

have sworn allegiance to Mary Magdalene), and the face below is a Green Man*, although it is difficult to see any vegetation emanating from its gaping mouth. Either way, what is this doing on a Catholic chapel?

When you stand inside the entrance to the chapel, notice the numerous Templar crosses/Order of Christ crosses and the armillary sphere* laid in mosaic in the floor. On the ceiling directly overhead is an eye emblazoned within a triangle, set in the cross of the Order of Christ, which in turn is set on a medallion of numerous rays of light (God's radiance?). This triangle-surrounded eye is also found on the US dollar bill.

In Christian iconography, this triangle represents the divine trinity of Father, Son, and Holy Spirit. Since the late 18th century, the eye has been used to represent the Eye of Divine Providence, indicative of God's compassionate watchfulness over humanity, although its origins go back to the Eye of Horus, a protective Egyptian amulet. In Masonic symbolism, this symbol is called the Delta Radiant and represents the All-seeing Eye of the Great Architect of the Universe. The triangle can also refer to the three alchemical materials: sulfur, mercury, and salt.

"If there's a place in Portugal where the myth or reality of the Underground World is presented with all its might…this place is right here, at Quinta da Regaleira de Sintra, which has already been recognized as the Holy Mountain since the dawn of human civilization…" Vitor Manuel Adrião^, p. 243.

Gruta do Labirinto/The Labyrinth Lake and Grotto, and the House of Thoth

This charming, artificial lake hides secrets: the greenery-dripping entrance at one end of the landing above the lake opens onto a flight of stairs that disappears into darkness. The underground passage leads to a rocky grotto and vistas of ducks preening themselves on the lake. The path continues up and down,  into darkness and back into light, before surfacing at the other side of the lake. Bring a flashlight or use your smartphone to avoid losing your footing.

Just past the lake is the Casa dos Ibis/House of Thoth/Balnearium Fountain/Ibis Fountain. The building was there before Carvalho Monteiro bought the Quinta and served as the garden's washrooms. It was converted into a fountain filled with hermetic symbolism. The two sacred ibis symbolize Thoth (the Greek Hermes), the Egyptian god of divine wisdom, giver of knowledge and writing. The Egyptian lotus

flowers represent purity and are the material used for making papyrus. The meaning of the snake hiding in the flowers and caught in the ibis's beak is open to interpretation.

Poço Iniciático/Initiatic Well

The Initiatic Well, also called an inverted tower, is built near the highest elevation of the Quinta. It is not a well, however. It is an inverted tower that extends into the earth to a depth of 30 m (98 ft). It was never intended for water; rather, it is a well to plumb the depths of the initiate's progress. In other words, it might have been used for initiatic rituals (neo-Templar? Masonic? Rosicrucian?), though nobody is sure. Whatever its real purpose, the enigmatic well provides ample sustenance for the imagination. It opens into an underground passageway.

Tourists enter the well from the top through a secret door in a faux dolmen* constructed of moss-covered boulders. The entrance is oriented to the north, the direction associated with wisdom in esoteric traditions. The northern orientation also ensures that the well does not receive a lot of direct sunlight, thus shrouding its interior in shadows. The dolmen is a reference to prehistoric burial monuments and (literally) sets the stage for what is to come—an initiatic journey that takes one from death to spiritual rebirth, into darkness and back out to the light.

A spiraling staircase divided into nine landings winds around the inside of the well. According to some researchers, the number nine is a reference to the nine levels of initiation in the Knights Templar hierarchy—if there were such levels. Or perhaps the number nine refers to the nine-month human gestation period, at the end of which the fetus  leaves the womb (exits the initiatic well) and moves through the birth canal (one of the underground passages) to be born (or reborn) into the light.

The official CulturSintra brochure (available for purchase in the gift shop) asserts there are ten landings, not nine, and the number 10 is a reference to the final part of Dante's Divine Comedy. After Dante ascends with Beatrix to the ninth sphere of Paradise, he is led by Saint Bernard to the tenth level, the Empyrean Heaven.

Between each of the nine landings are 15 steps, which add up to 135, which can be converted (1+3+5) to nine. The CulturSintra brochure, however, counts 10 landings and 139 steps. 1+3+9 can be converted to 13, which is said to symbolize death and rebirth, the culmination of the journey of initiation, as well as a reference to the Death Card (#13) in the Tarot deck.

Neo-Romanesque arches on columns frame the spiraling way, and their carved capitols tease us with secret symbolism. References to the Zodiac? To the seven chakras? Imaginative theorists have suggested many possibilities. A line of 22 niches spirals down the side of the staircase opening into the center of the well. These niches have been interpreted as a reference to the 22 Major Arcana cards of the Tarot deck, which is also interpreted as an initiatic journey.

If you wish to descend into the well as a kind of mini-initiatic journey, it is best to go there when it isn't filled with tourists. Early in the morning during the week is a better time than late morning on Saturday. Once you arrive outside the well, take time to center yourself before you enter. For further assistance, use the BLESSING acronym on p. 10. Maintain silence. An initiatic journey can be challenging. Be cautious: the Initiatic Well is damp and dark, and the staircase can be slippery.

On the floor at the bottom of the well is a mosaic compass laid over a Templar's Cross. Or perhaps it is a Cross Pattée, a reference to an engraving in a 17th-century alchemy manual, where the cross is called the Sign of the Adepts. The base portico is flanked by columns. To the right as you exit is a water vase and font, originally used for ritual purification.

The well opens into a labyrinth of tunnels. The compass points to the passageway that forks toward the eastern entrance and to the Lake of the Cascade with its waterfall, narrow bridge, and 15 stepping-stones—the same number as steps between landings

in the Well. The Waterfall Lake is a reference to the Classical Greek River Styx, the mythological underground river that forms the boundary between this world and the Underworld.

It is also suggestive of the Styx Lake described by the famous Portuguese poet Luís Vaz de Camões^* (1525–1580), whose epic poetry and rare editions were highly prized by Carvalho Monteiro. The open grotto was constructed from local granite rocks,

basalt, and imported coral, uniting minerals associated with the alchemical elements of fire, earth, and water. Perhaps the tumbling waterfall evokes the fourth element, air.

A fork in the underground passageway on the right leads to the Imperfect Well, a 9 m (30 ft) deep inverted

tower. It is a much cruder structure and may have been built in the 1830s by the previous owner Manuel Bernardo Fernandes, who was probably a Freemason.

After wandering in the dark through the tunnels, the initiates would arrive at the Imperfect Well. But here they would discover that they could not climb up to reach the surface. The way is blocked and the stairway leads nowhere. Apparently, this was to indicate to the initiate that spiritual progress has to be internal, not external, and is not based on material things. As you wander above-ground through the park, you come to the Imperfect Well, which is surrounded by a metal fence. You can look down into it.

Eventually the underground passageway leads to the Grotto of the East and opens onto the surface.

The journey described above starts at the top of the Initiatic Well and descends spiraling clockwise, goes through the tunnels, reaches the lake, passing by the Imperfect Well, and traverses the length of the subterranean passageway until reaching the exit at

the Grotto of the East. This is the way the current tourist itinerary requires you to go. (Note: Not all the tunnels are currently open to the public.)

However, the creator of the Quinta probably intended the journey to start at the other end. One would begin at the Grotto of the East, nestled at the base of tall trees. One would enter the underground passage, which heads east to west, pass the Imperfect Well with no exit, cross the stepping stones at Cascade Lake, ascend the Initiatic Well in a counter-clockwise direction, and emerge at

the highest point, closer to Heaven and, perhaps, to spiritual elevation.

Another underground passageway is hidden behind a curtain of water at the Portal of the Guardians. The entrance is guarded by two hybrid beings who defend the passage between the two worlds (known/unknown, light/dark, physical/spiritual, above/below, World of Appearance/World of Essence). This tunnel leads not to the base entrance of the Initiatic Well but to an entrance on the fourth landing, halfway between the base floor and the ground floor. If these landings relate to the seven (or more) chakras, this entrance is situated at the level of the heart chakra. The landing faces west, and in many traditions, the west is the direction of compassion and love.

As you descend the well, notice what you feel. Tingly? Queasy? Elated? Elyn found herself shaking, and it wasn't just from the effort of trying not to slip on the stone steps. She described it later as "feeling the powerful energy that has accumulated inside the well from its use as an initiatic journey." The spiral, like a coiled spring, stores energy.

Getting There/Other Information

The Quinta is a 10-minute (750 m/0.5 mi) walk from the National Palace in the Historic Center. Walk past the palace towards the Tourist Office. It has a large banner in front advertising the informative and entertaining, multimedia "Sintra—Mitos e Lendas" (Myths and Legends of Sintra). Take the road to the left and follow it out of town, heading toward the right. The road is relatively flat until the final 320 m (0.2 mi). You will pass a large fountain and waterfall (Cascata dos Pisões) on the left, and soon you will see the high walls that surround the Quinta.

When you get to the large iron gates on the left and a small road on the right, you have reached the exit to the Quinta. The road then goes uphill to the entrance and ticket office. Tickets can be purchased there or online. Make sure to pick up a map of the

Quinta, although there are frequent signposts along the main pathway that meanders through the grounds. Remember: especially in Quinta da Regaleira, the map is not the territory. The map doesn't include the elevation of the different sites, but it does show a number of trails and shortcuts from the main path. The Initiatic Well is near the top of the map and near the highest point in the Quinta. Figuring out where you are can be confusing, but it's probably supposed to be.

Informative audio devices can be rented at the ticket desk. Hold the device parallel to the ground, white side up, and point the end at the black box on the information posts scattered along the main path. They are marked on the map with a headphones icon.

There are toilets near the entrance, the cafeteria, and en route to the Initiatic Well. The cafeteria includes outdoor seating and offers daily lunchtime specials as well as snacks and light refreshment. The gift shop is in the lower level of the palace. Check open hours if it is important to you to visit the shop. It sells souvenir merchandise and specialized books about the Quinta.

http://www.regaleira.pt/en/

GPS: 38°47'45.15"N, 9°23'50.21"W

Nearby Sites to Explore

The Palácio de Seteais/ Seteais Palace

If you continue walking up the street past the Quinta entrance—perhaps a 3-minute walk—you will see a sign on the right pointing to the Palace of Seteais. This is an impressive 18th-century palace that is now a 5-star Tivoli hotel. You can enter the grounds and enjoy the view through the large archway that divides the two main buildings. You can also enter the hotel and go to the bar on the lower level (lovely views, less

expensive than the restaurant) or splurge on a meal in the dining room.

Address: Rua Barbosa du Bocage 8, 2710-517 Sintra.

Casa do Fauno

Casa do Fauno is a café located in the heart of the Mountain of the Moon, in Quinta dos Lobos, in what was once part of the ancient Forest of Almosquer. Dom Afonso Henriques gave this land to the Knights Templar* in the 12th century, so it is deeply rooted in history.

Casa do Fauno is a contemporary take on a medieval pub, something like "Renaissance Faire meets Society for Creative Anachronism." Although access to the Templar-trod, mythical forest is restricted, you can sit inside or outside the pub, sip an espresso or a glass of mead, have a sandwich or dessert, listen to live music, and soak in the atmosphere. Upstairs is Ishtar—Artes Mágicas, a small shop specializing in crystals, incense, pagan and witchcraft items, and esoteric books (most if not

all in Portuguese). Ishtar hosts book signings and interesting workshops.

Getting There

The Casa is about 1.3 km (0.8 mi) from the National Palace of Sintra. If you walk from the Sintra Historic Center toward Quinta da Regaleira, when you reach the Quinta exit gates, you will be almost halfway there. Instead of continuing up the road, turn right onto the Rua da Trindade Coelho, a narrow road that looks at first glance like a parking lot. The sign says *rua sem saida* (road without exit), but the road has an exit and changes its name to Caminho dos Frades. Continue walking down the road about 400 m (1/4 mi) until on the corner on the left you see the white-walled entrance to Casa do Fauno. The pub is usually open from late afternoon until very late at night. It offers Portuguese pub food, various kinds of drinks, and live music.

Address: Casa do Fauno, Quinta dos Lobos, 1, Caminho dos Frades (400 m/ 1/4 mi from Quinta da Regaleira), 2710-560 Sintra

Casa do Fauno

For more information, go to https:// casadofauno.wordpress.com/

Castelo dos Mouros/Castle of the Moors

"As we walked up the path to the Moorish Castle, perched on top of Sintra Mountain, I could feel an intense 'buzzing' static charge emanating from the immense granite boulders that litter the sides of the hill. The huge, moss-covered boulders reeked with energy. It was so strong it created a visual distortion that resembled heat rising from the pavement on a scorching summer day. Everything was slightly out of focus. Whew. I couldn't imagine living here, but people have been drawn to this high point on the Mountain of the Moon for more than 7,000 years." —Elyn

Background

The massive stone walls of the Moorish Castle snake over the even more massive granite boulders that litter the sides of Sintra Mountain. Colorful flags wave from the castle's parapets, silhouetted against the sky on a sunny day. Suddenly, fog rolls in and it all disappears. Fog rolls out and the castle appears again,

a fairytale fortress perched on top of the Monte da Lua. It is the only castle in the Sintra UNESCO World Heritage Site; the others are all palaces.

The Moorish Castle was built somewhere between the 9th and 11th centuries. It is an irregularly shaped military outpost, constructed on an exposed, rocky granite outcrop at an elevation of 450 m (1476 ft) on a summit of Sintra Mountain. There are two sets of walls, 450 m of meandering battlements within the inner wall, and 13 defensive towers. In places it seems as if the castle is not separate from the bedrock but grows out of it like something organic.

With its expansive views of surrounding territory and the coastline, the castle was built as a defensive center for the vast agricultural region in the extreme west of Garb al-Andalus*. To withstand sieges, the Moors constructed a vast rainwater cistern (18 m long by 6 m wide, and 6 m high) inside the castle walls. The cistern was so well constructed that it continued to provide water to the town of Sintra until the 1910s.

Arab chroniclers describe the rich fertile lands of Sintra and list the Castelo dos Mouros as one of the most important in the region, more important even than the castle in Lisbon. As part of the Reconquest*, the castle was captured in 1093 by a small Christian army, but they could not keep it for long. It was conquered at last by Dom Afonso Henriques in 1147.

The Moors weren't the first to occupy this particular hilltop on the Monte da Lua, nor were they the last. Archaeological digs have discovered human habitation dating back at least 7,000 years. Neolithic artifacts have been found in all the excavations around the castle. Many other communities also settled here, and archaeologists have found evidence dating to the Copper, Bronze, and Iron Ages, as well as proof of commercial ties with the Phoenicians and Romans.

The Moors took over this choice location (good water, shade, excellent overview of the surrounding area) in the ninth century during their invasion of Iberia. The Muslim conquerors built houses, an oven, and silos for storing grains and legumes on the sheltered, southeastern slope of the hill. Typical Islamic artifacts have been found there, along with the remains of deer, sheep, goats, wild boar, and fox, as well as broad beans, and peach, plum, and olive stones.

Dom Afonso Henriques conquered the castle without a battle in 1147—the Moorish inhabitants simply walked away without a fight. He destroyed the Muslim quarter and built a Christian cemetery over the site. Next to it, he built the Church of São Pedro de Canaferrim, the first of four parish churches he constructed in Sintra. The church was built between the inner and outer walls of the castle, and was used for worship until at least the 15th century.

In 1154, less than a decade after taking possession of the castle, Dom Afonso Henriques bestowed it (and the town of Sintra) upon Gualdim Pais, Master of the Templar Order in Portugal. A Christian community of 30 people was settled in the castle and worshipped in the church. That group left in the early 15th century, if not before, in order to be closer to Sintra town. With the success of the Reconquest*, the castle was no longer needed as a lookout post.

It is possible that at some time in the 15th century a Sephardic* Jewish community may have established itself in the now-vacant castle. There are unclear references about Jewish use of the castle and abandoned chapel. The Jews were expelled from Portugal in 1497.

By the end of the 15th century, the castle was completely abandoned and falling into disrepair. The Lisbon earthquake of 1755 didn't help its state of conservation, either. The castle lay in ruins until 1839, at which time Dom Fernando II (who was also responsible for building nearby Pena Palace) began the lengthy process of reconstructing what was left of the castle walls and restoring some of the castle, a process that has continued ever since.

Dom Fernando II's restoration project was designed to create a "keep-landscape," a romanticized evocation of the past, a mixture of "contemplative ruined castle keep" and pleasure garden. The castle is visible from

Pena Palace, and he wanted it to form part of Pena Park's romantic "natural" scenery.

The castle that we see today appears to be an intact medieval fortress, but appearances are deceiving. And although it is called the Castle of the Moors, it hasn't been that for nearly a millennium. The impressive crenelated and turreted double set of walls are actually a mixture of medieval Moorish architecture (10th to 12th centuries), 12th to 13th century Christian repairs, romantic 19th century restoration (under Dom Fernando II), and 20th-century interventions by the General Directorate of Buildings and Monuments.

The king's renovation works partially destroyed the medieval Christian necropolis located next to the Church of São Pedro de Canaferrim, so he had a small tomb built in which to lay the remains that had been disturbed. The inscription on the monument bears both a crescent and a cross, and this epitaph: "What man has assembled only God can set apart." Meaning that they could not distinguish whether the remains were Christian or Muslim.

Although today the hillside is covered with massive trees and exuberant vegetation, that, too, is a fairly modern alteration. The original forest was destroyed long ago, due to agricultural practices, forestry, and the use of the land for pasture. Dom Fernando II changed that by bringing his romantic sensibility to the environment, an aesthetic that delighted in carefully constructed "natural-looking" landscapes. This can be seen in its fullest expression at Pena Palace, which includes the large Park of Pena, of which the Moorish Castle forms a visual part.

Since 1976, the castle has been the site of numerous archaeological excavations. In 1995, it became part of the Sintra UNESCO World Heritage Cultural Landscape Site. And in 2000, Parques de Sintra took over management of the site.

What to Explore

Markers along the route provide information in Portuguese and English about select points of interest. The path itself is delightful, lined with massive, moss-covered, ivy-draped granite boulders, sheer cliffs, huge trees, strategically placed benches, and occasional mini-gardens—all designed to look perfectly natural or, if possible, to even improve on nature.

Before walking up to the castle, consciously begin your journey. Remember that people have inhabited this hillside for 7,000 years or more, living and dying here, leaving behind traces of their histories and their experiences—and even their bodies. Ask permission of the resident "guardians of the land*." Sense, see, and feel how the landscape impacts you as you walk slowly up to the massive stone ramparts. Do you sense the energy of the land itself, expressed in the granite boulders and the dense forest? Imagine what it might have been like to live here millennia ago.

As you walk up the wide cobblestone path to the castle, past the outer ring of walls, you will come to the medieval Church of São Pedro de Canaferrim, which now serves as the interpretation center for the history of castle. There is an audiovisual show, (sometimes) interactive exhibits, and display cases full of various artifacts discovered during archaeological digs.

Next door to the church is a large wood and plexiglass construction that allows you to see some of what was uncovered during archaeological excavations at the site. You can see finds from as long ago as 7,000 years and as recent as the Islamic quarter and Christian necropolis.

As you keep walking up the hill, you will reach the castle's impressive inner walls. Inside is the cistern, the castle keep, and the so-called royal tower, among other attractions. One of the main attractions is the view, so if the day is clear, a walk on the parapets is well worthwhile. And if it's foggy—well, that only adds to the mystique.

Getting There/Other Information

The castle is approximately 1.4 km (0.87 mi) from downtown Sintra and 1.7 km (1 mi) from the train station, but it's all uphill and a stiff, though attractive, climb by road or trail. The castle is approximately 210 m (690 ft) above Sintra town.

One option is to take motorized transport up to the castle and then walk down. The hop-on hop-off Scotturb bus 434, hop-on hop-off CitySightSeeing buses, tuk-tuks, and taxis take you to the entrances to the Moorish Castle and nearby Pena Palace, which are only 200 m (0.12 mi) apart. They stop near the main ticket office. Tickets are required and lines can be long, so schedule your visit early or later in the day.

The wide paved path leads from the ticket office uphill to the castle, passing through the outer ring of walls before reaching the 19th-century tomb marker, the chapel/interpretive center, and the necropolis/Islamic quarter excavation. A little further uphill you reach the castle's inner ring of walls. There is another ticket office, a gift shop, WC, and a cafe.

If you want to walk up to (or down from) the castle, there are two routes, the Caminho de Santa Maria or the steeper Vila Sassetti hiking trail, which also go to Pena Palace. It helps to consult Google or Apple maps to find your way.

If you take the Caminho de Santa Maria, there are many places to start. If you are in the Sintra historic center, take Rua Mal. Saldanha, which becomes

Calçada dos Clérigos, or the parallel street, Rua Visc. de Monserrate (the street that goes past Ale-Hop and the NewsMuseum), out of town to the Church of Santa Maria. If you take the Rua Visc. de Monserrate, you will have to take a set of stairs on the right called Escadinhas dos Clérigos to join up with the Calçada dos Clérigos. When you join up with the Calçada, you turn left onto it and soon arrive at the Church of Santa Maria.

The Church of Santa Maria is one of the four original parish churches, first built in the 12th century by Dom Afonso Henriques. It bears a resemblance to the Templar church Santa Maria do Olival in Tomar*. This church is considered the main Gothic-style church in Sintra and has been a listed National Monument since 1922. It is usually closed, but if you are fortunate enough to enter, spend some time quietly near the altar in the rounded apse*. It has a very sweet energy. The custodian, Paula, told us, "It's round like the womb of Mary, where the body of Christ [the communion] takes form."

Just past the church you will come to Casa do Adro. The house has a plaque on it stating that Hans

Christian Andersen^ stayed there briefly in 1866. Then, on the right you come to a cobbled street and a sign, "To the Castelo dos Mouros." The short but very steep paved road (Rampa do Castelo) continues past the Church of São Miguel on the right. This church was one of the original four medieval parish churches and collapsed during the 1755 Lisbon earthquake. All that was left was the apse. Dom Fernando II in the mid-19th century turned the apse* of the church into a housing space, perhaps to provide housing closer to the work being done on Pena Palace.

Continuing uphill, you pass through an impressive, ivy-covered stone archway. The wide cobblestone path continues up the hill in a series of switchbacks through the forest. Conveniently placed benches enable hikers to catch their breath at scenic locations. A mixture of ramps and steps, the path eventually leads to the 19th-century tomb marker, the ruined church/interpretive center, the necropolis/Islamic quarter excavation, and the ticket office/gift shop/cafe.

The Moorish Castle

https://www.parquesdesintra.pt/en/parks-monuments/the-moorish-castle/

https://www.parquesdesintra.pt/media/pspaaztf/brochura_percursos_pedestres.pdf

https://cdn.elebase.io/173fe953-8a63-4a8a-8ca3-1bacb56d78a5/5d16efd1-4b5b-43ef-b4a9-d263a41403ce-sintra-hiking-trails.pdf

GPS: 38°47'24.25"N, 9°23'21.47"W

Parque e Palácio da Pena/Park and Palace of Pena

"The 'jewel in the crown of Dom Fernando II, the Artist King' is an over-the-top confection perched on top of the second highest spot on the Monte da Lua. The palace's excesses are the expression of an exuberantly romantic imagination. That's not necessarily a bad thing. It just depends on your taste. The extensive park is an alluring mixture of nature and artifice, of natural and artificial. Strolling through the carefully constructed landscape offers the opportunity to step into a fairytale." —Elyn

Background

Buried beneath the romantic exotica of Pena Palace lies a very different story, a story that is less fairytale and more religious. Sometime before the 12th century, an apparition of the Virgin Mary was reported on this rocky crag (*penha*) on the Monte da Lua by a shepherdess. In 1372, a chapel was built there by Henrique Manuel de Vilhena, Count of Seia e Sintra, uncle of Dom Fernando I, because of the local discovery of a miraculous image related to the 12th-century apparition. In 1493, Dom João II and his wife Dona Leanor made a pilgrimage to the chapel to fulfill a vow and in mourning for the death of their son, Prince Afonso.

On November 10, 1503, Dom João's successor, Dom Manuel I, was hunting a white deer in the mountain. From a high vantage point, Dom Manuel I saw the arrival in Cascais of the fleet of nine vessels commanded by Vasco da Gama—the (now diminished in number) armada he had sent the previous year to India.

A white deer is a rare and unusual animal that has important symbolic meaning. Celtic people believed that a white deer was a messenger from the spirit world, and Christians associate the white stag with Christ. White is a symbol of purity and also of light conquering darkness. Perhaps the king was not actually hunting a white deer but, instead, seeking spiritual guidance.

In thanksgiving for the return of the fleet, Dom Manuel I erected the monastery of Nossa Senhora da Pena in the same place as the earlier chapel. At an elevation of 480 m (1575 ft), it is the second highest point on Sintra Mountain. (The highest point is nearby and marked by a high cross.)

Because of the king's devotion to St. Jerome, he donated the monastery in 1511 to the Hieronymite (St. Jerome) Order, a Catholic cloistered religious order. It was a small monastic community, settled in a quiet place for meditation, with a maximum of 22 monks.

The 1755 Lisbon earthquake devastated the monastery, but it remained functioning until the 1834 abolition of religious orders. After the monks left, the monastery fell into disrepair. Some evidence of their long occupation can still be seen in the park, for example, the Grotto of the Monk, where they went for retreat.

In 1836, Dona Marie II married Ferdinand of Saxe-Coburg and Gotha (1816–1885), a prince who was nephew to Leopold I of Belgium and first cousin of British Prince Albert and Queen Victoria. According to the nuptial contract, after the birth of their first son, he was given the status of king-consort and became Dom Fernando II.

Dom Fernando II was a highly cultured man, a true "Artist King." He spoke many languages and was thoroughly educated in the arts, especially music and drawing. He was deeply interested in the romantic

aesthetic of the time, so popular in his Germanic homeland. He was also an artist, a collector, and a patron of the arts.

He fell in love with Sintra and the Mountain of the Moon. Using his own funds, he acquired the now-ruined Hieronymite Monastery in 1838 and began to transform it. The 16th-century ruined monastery, often swathed in fog and buffeted by high winds, held a fascination for him that grew out of his cultural background and his Germanic romantic sensibility, which was fascinated by "the sublime," nature, ruins, and the exotic.

All over the world, new religious buildings are constructed on top of old ones devoted to a previous faith. The Basilica of Our Lady of Guadalupe in Mexico City is built over an Aztec holy place dedicated to an Aztec mother goddess. In France, Chartres Cathedral is built over an ancient Celtic sacred site and holy well, and the cathedral in Le Puy-en-Velay is built over an ancient dolmen. Pena Palace incorporates a monastery that was built over a chapel of Our Lady of Pena. Monserrate Palace (see p. 99) was also built over a chapel, and, like Pena Palace, was built in homage to Romanticism, not religion.

Dom Fernando II's original plan in 1838 was to create a royal summer residence by remodeling what remained of the Hieronymite monastery. These rooms included the cloister, dining room, sacristy, chapel, and bell tower, and they are what are known as the Old Palace, which he had painted a dusty pink.

By 1843, the king had decided to expand the palace by creating a new wing, known as the New Palace, painted a yellow ochre, which includes the Great Hall, a circular tower, and a new kitchen. Work

continued into the 1860s. The eclectic styles include neo-Manueline, neo-Islamic, neo-Renaissance, and fantasized medieval. Circling the main building are other architectural structures in keeping with the romantic and faux-medieval aesthetic: parapet walks, towers, and a drawbridge, to name a few.

What is it about this *penha* of the Monte da Lua that has drawn people for centuries? First, there was the Apparition of the Virgin, then a chapel dedicated to Our Lady of Pena, then the Hieronymite Monastery. Perhaps Dom Fernando also sensed some spiritual energy emanating from the rocky crag.

The extensive (200 hectares) woodland park enabled Fernando II to further develop the romantic style, in this case combining exoticism and nature in the form of carefully placed pavilions, temples, fountains,

gardens, groves, miradors, and lakes, enhanced with botanical specimens imported from all over the world, including Portugal. He worked with the architect Baron de Eschwege and the engineer Baron Kessler to draw plans for the entire parkland, respecting the uneven terrain, the soil, the climate, and taking advantage of the amazing views—including the palace, which is visible from any point.

Diverse contrasting environments, surprising and exotic features, lakes connected via waterfalls, Japanese cedars, New Zealand ferns, North American sequoia, magnolia, tree ferns from New Zealand, cedars of Lebanon—a total of 2,000 species were brought in to create a multi-sensory romanticized virtual reality that attempted to simulate (if not create) a perfect state of nature. A series of paths and narrow roads provided access to different areas.

Dona Maria II died in 1853 during the birth of their eleventh child. Because of Portuguese law, Dom Fernando was no longer king; his son became king and he became regent. Fernando continued to live in Pena Palace, and it continued to be used by other members of the Royal Family.

In 1860, the widowed regent met Elise Hensler, a talented and highly educated opera singer who later became Countess of Edla. She also lived in the palace, perhaps beginning in 1865, and she began contributing to the ongoing design of the palace and park. In 1864, they built the Alpine-inspired Chalet of the Countess of Edla in Pena Park. They married in 1869.

After Fernando's death in 1885, the palace passed to the Countess of Edla. She sold the palace to Fernando's son, Dom Luis, who wished to retrieve it for the royal family. Fernando's children continued to spend time in the Palace. Dom Carlos I (1863–1908) and Dona Amelia of Orleans (1865–1951) spent summers there. Their son, Manuel II, maintained chambers in the main floor of the (Royal) Tower in the New Palace.

Dona Amelia was in Pena Palace when she received word of the Declaration of the Republic on October 5, 1910. Together with her mother-in-law Maria Pia and her son, Manuel, they departed from nearby Ericeira in the royal yacht and sailed for Gibraltar.

Pena Palace was classified as a National Monument in 1910 and is perhaps the most important (or at least the most visited) attraction in the Sintra UNESCO World Heritage Site. Over time, the original bright red and yellow façades had faded to gray, but during late 20th-century restorations, the exterior of the palace was restored to its original colors. In 2007, Parques de Sintra took over managing the palace, which has undergone constant conservation and restoration work. It is considered one of the Seven Wonders of Portugal and one of the major expressions of 19th-century Romanticism in the world. It is also used for State occasions by the President of the Portuguese Republic and other government officials.

What to Explore

The immense park and fairytale palace provide much to experience. The Old Palace, with its smaller, more domestic rooms, has a very different "feel" than the New Palace, intended for public display and official events. There is wonderful tilework, organic twining vines on the balustrades, elaborate trompe l'oeil murals, geometric neo-Mudejar* patterns on some of the walls and ceilings. Each room is different. Once you enter the palace, you must follow the visitor route.

A few outstanding attractions include the terraces, with stunning views of the surrounding hills. Before entering the palace itself, visit the Terrace of the Triton, with its huge carving of a mythological triton—part human, part fish—emerging from a conch shell, perhaps symbolizing the allegory of the creation of the world. Or perhaps it symbolizes the Transmutation of Species. Or maybe it alludes to *The Lusiads,* by Luís Vaz de Camões^, in which the Triton is associated with the theme of the Age of Discovery.

The Chapel (entered from the Courtyard of Arches, behind the Triton Terrace): This space is the one that has remained most unchanged since the time of the Monastery of Pena. It includes a magnificent 16th-century alabaster and black limestone altarpiece attributed to the French sculptor Nicolas de Chantereine. Also of note is the stained-glass window in the chapel nave, commissioned by Dom Fernando II in 1840. The windows reference the history of the Monastery of Pena.

Once you are inside the palace, your visit begins with the Royal Family Dining Room. Dom Fernando II adapted the former rectory of the monastery and turned it into the royal pantry and dining room. The room, with its vaulted Manueline ribbed ceiling, became the private family dining room. The table setting and fruit arrangements are the same as they would have been during royal habitation.

The Manueline Cloister

Constructed in 1511, it is small and intimate, reflecting the size of the religious community that lived here. In the center is a conch shell similar to the shell of the Triton. The walls are covered with attractive, geometric-patterned Hispano-Mudéjar tiles. Dom Fernando II turned

the 14 cells in the upper level into domestic spaces, including his master bedroom.

The Office of King Carlos (1863–1908)

This occupies what was formerly the Chapter House of the Hieronymite monastery. Most notable is the painted fabric mural depicting nymphs and fawns in Pena Park, painted by Dom Carlos, who took up residence in the lower floor of the Manueline cloister. It was left unfinished because he was assassinated in Lisbon on Feb. 1, 1908. The next room was the king's bathroom, reflecting advances in hygiene in the 19th century.

The Master Bedroom of Ferdinand II

With its richly canopied bed, vaulted ceiling, and decorated walls, this was the main bedroom in the palace. The neo-Mudéjar* geometric-design painted stucco was completed in 1882, reflecting Fernando's romantic aesthetic incorporating the Islamic heritage of Portugal. Fernando had planned chambers for himself and Dona Maria II in the Turret Tower, but the queen died before its completion. The king decided to remain in this room in the old

convent*, with a view of the Moorish Castle (see p. 73), which he altered to make more romantically appealing. Most unconventionally, the widowed Fernando cohabited with his companion and future wife, the Countess of Edla, in this bedroom.

The Magnificent Woodland Park

You mustn't miss a stroll through the park, which begins just past the ticket office near the road. (There is another entry at the Valley of Lakes.) Remade in the English style, it includes a variety of exotic tree species, delightful "stage settings" of wild groves, lakes, pavilions, faux dolmens, and much more,

including the Queen's Fern Valley and the Grotto of the Monk. The highest point on Sintra Mountain is 528 m (1732 ft); it is marked by a high cross in the park, first erected by João III around 1522 but later destroyed by a storm. It was later replaced by Dom Fernando II. That cross was destroyed by lightning, and in 2008 a new limestone cross was put in place. It is 3.5 m (11.5 ft) high and 1.5 m (5 ft) wide. The views are amazing. At the far west end of the park is the Chalet of the Condessa. Visiting time in the park, if you follow the 4–km sign-posted itinerary, is about 1 hour and 15 minutes, depending on how much you dawdle.

Getting There/Other Information

Perched at an elevation of 480 m (1575 ft) above Sintra town (elevation 190 m/623 ft), Pena Palace can be reached on foot, but it is a bit of a climb. Motorized vehicles are a much easier way to arrive, including Scotturb bus 434, CitySightSeeing buses, tuk-tuks, and taxis. Private vehicles are not permitted to drive to the palace because the road is quite narrow and traffic jams are not infrequent.

Pena Palace is a highly popular tourist attraction, so lines at the ticket office at the entrance can be very long. It is advisable to buy combined palace and park e-tickets in advance and arrive first thing in the morning (even before the palace opens) or later in the afternoon. Tickets are purchased for a specific entry time. Tickets for entrance to Pena Park can also be purchased separately. A ticket (purchased in advance or on site) is needed for the shuttle bus that will take you from the ticket office up the steep incline to the palace, saving both time and energy. Or you can walk up, following the road or the meandering paths.

If you take the shuttle bus, you will still need to climb a short distance on a wide cobblestone road in order to reach the entrance to the palace and the scenic terraces that surround it. There are a restaurant, a gift shop, and WC at the palace as well as at the ticket office near the road.

If you walk up to the Castle of the Moors (see p. 73), the entrance to Pena Palace is only a short distance further down the road.

Pena Palace

https://www.parquesdesintra.pt/en/parks-monuments/park-and-national-palace-of-pena/

GPS: 38°47'16.45"N, 9°23'15.35"W

Watch Gary's interview with Freddy Silva in Pena Park. It is about the founding of the state of Portugal by the Knights Templar.

https://youtu.be/iVuWZ6Rx6GU/

Interview with
Freddy Silva

Parque e Palácio de Monserrate/Monserrate Park and Palace

"We stumbled upon the so-called ruined chapel as we strolled through the extensive park. A rubber tree spread over the crumbling walls, vines wedged their roots between decaying stones, and verdant foliage adorned the interior spaces. It looked authentic but, in fact, it was faux, a romantic landscape ornament constructed in 1790. It evokes the idea of the supremacy of wild Nature over human endeavor—but in fact, Nature here is tamed. The real ruined chapel of Monserrate lies buried beneath the palace." —Elyn

Background

Monserrate Palace is a palatial villa, an eclectic and charming construction, designed with rotundas and towers, arabesque cut-outs and Moorish-influenced plaster work. There's even a fountain in the center of the palace. The extensive English gardens* are delightful. It is hard to imagine that it was a hotbed of espionage during World War II (see p. 105).

Local legends assert that the land was first settled when an ancient chapel was built here over the tomb of a noble Christian knight killed during the Reconquest*. Or perhaps a chapel to the Virgin Mary was built here by Dom Afonso Henriques after his reconquest of Sintra in 1147. Or perhaps those are really two versions of the same event. At any rate, it's probable that humans settled here centuries before the chapel was built because the irrigation system appears to be of Moorish origin.

Long after the Reconquest*, the land was sold to the Hospital Real de Todos os Santos in Lisbon, which was founded in 1508. Friar Gaspar Preto, the rector of the hospital, went on pilgrimage to the shrine of Our Lady of Montserrat in Catalonia, Spain. On his return, he felt inspired to construct a chapel here in 1540 in her honor, perhaps because he perceived a similarity between the Portuguese Sintra Serra and the Catalan "Mont Serrat" (serrated ridged mountain). He had an alabaster effigy of the Virgin of Montserrat placed in the chapel. He also planned to use the estate as a workshop and for growing products to be used in the hospital.

> Two chapels dedicated to Our Lady? What is it about this place that evokes such dedication?

The estate of Monserrate was acquired in 1718 by Caetano de Mello e Castro, Commander of Christ (a reference to the Order of Christ, which replaced the Knights Templar* in Portugal) and Viceroy of India. The site was partly devastated by the 1755 Lisbon earthquake, which destroyed the estate's farmhouses. In 1789 it was rented by Gerard de Visme, a wealthy British trader. He ordered the construction of a neo-Gothic palace over the ruins of the former

Monserrate Chapel. It was similar in style to the hermitage (the so-called ruined chapel) in the garden, which he had built. He also began developing gardens in the English manner. He lived there only a few years before abruptly returning to England.

In 1793 or 1794 the exceedingly wealthy British writer William Beckford rented Monserrate. He began restoration projects on Visme's villa and started to design the extensive landscaped garden with imported specimens. He left in 1798 or 1799 and the place fell into ruin. But it was a very romantic ruin, and it soon gained a reputation as a romantic attraction.

Lord Byron^ visited in 1809 and wrote about it in his epic poem *Childe Harold's Pilgrimage*. He describes "Cintra's glorious Eden" and likens it to the Elysian Fields of Greek mythology. He proclaims Monserrate a place where kings had visited but now the halls are deserted, the doors gape wide. In Romantic-inclined circles, Monserrate became known as a place of ruined splendor. Soon a visit to Monserrate became obligatory for foreign visitors, especially British. Many of them wrote about it in their travel accounts.

After a number of other owners attempted their own restorations and then abandoned the estate, in 1856 the wealthy British trader and art collector Francis Cook (1818–1901) sublet the estate. At that time, the abandoned castle was a wreck, as were Beckford's gardens. In 1863, Cook became the owner of the Estate of Monserrate and in 1870 the First Viscount of Monserrate. (He also bought the Capuchos Convent in 1873, see p. 110.)

Working with the architect James Thomas Knowles and James Knowles Jr. (father and son), Cook constructed the delightful palace that we see today over the remains of Visme's house. The building was finished in 1865 or 1866, about 10 years after the Palace and Park of Pena, and it shared in the same romanticism that was prevalent at that time. It is a combination of neo-Gothic and East Indian

influences, along with references to Moorish design features. The Islamic architectural style is a nod both to Romanticism and to the Islamic heritage of Sintra, referring back to the centuries when it was part of Al-Andalus*.

With the help of master landscapers, Cook's romantic sensibilities transformed the park into one of the finest of Portuguese gardens. The park is 50 hectares (124 acres) and includes carefully created landscaped gardens surrounded by a semi-natural oak forest. Different areas are devoted to different regions and themes (the Fern Garden, the Mexican Garden, the Rose Garden, etc.).

The diminutive palace was intended as a holiday home for the Cook family, a place they would visit twice a year for periods up to one month. Friends were invited to attend huge parties, but, for the most part, they stayed in nearby locations that Cook purchased in the Serra. Monserrate was also a place where part of Cook's very impressive art collection was to be displayed.

At the death of Francis Cook, his eldest son Frederick inherited the palace, titles, and aesthetic sensibilities. Later, his son, Herbert Cook, inherited the house and added to the important art collection. But World War I impacted the family business, and in 1928 Monserrate was put up for sale. A buyer was hard to find, given the economic crisis of 1929. With no buyers, in 1937 Herbert invited his son's friend Walter Kingsbury to manage the estate.

Kingsbury and his wife enjoyed an almost idyllic life at the estate until the outbreak of World War II. Portugal remained neutral, but that didn't mean the English living there couldn't help the British war effort. During the conflict, the palace became a staging post for artists, journalists, diplomats—and others—fleeing from the Nazis. Monserrate also became a center of intrigue. It hosted the British writer and spy, Malcolm Muggeridge, and at least one dinner at the palace was used to disseminate false information to an important Nazi sympathizer.

After the war ended, the fourth baronet, Francis Ferdinand Cook, put the estate up for sale again. In 1946, an auction was held, during which many of the palace's furnishings were dispersed. It was purchased in 1947 by a Portuguese businessman. Two years later, the Portuguese government acquired the estate, and in 1978 it was classified as a property in the Public

Interest. In 2000, management (and restoration and renovation) of the Park was taken over by Parques de Sintra; in 2007, it took over management of the Palace as well. The palace was reopened to the public in 2010 and has now been restored completely to its former appearance. In 2013, the Park of Monserrate was honored with a European Garden Award. The Park and Palace of Monserrate is a part of the Sintra UNESCO World Heritage Site.

What to Explore

Numerous signposts point the way on the garden trails and give distances to various attractions.

The Park

The botanical gardens are the result of four generations of master gardeners (1856–1947). It is designed in an English romantic style, including a lake, fountains,

grottoes, and 3,000 botanical specimens from all over the world. Plants are organized by geographical areas. Araucaria, palm trees, and tree ferns from Australia and New Zealand form one zone. The Mexican Garden, full of agaves and yuccas, forms another. Camellias, azaleas, rhododendrons, and bamboos represent Japan. There is also a Rose Garden. The artificial horseshoe-shaped lake was once called the Hippocrene, after a legendary fountain in Ancient Greece where the Muses inspired poets. Beckford's Waterfall, also artificial, tumbles down the side of a verdant cliff, surrounded with botanical species, including the Himalayan Kahili Ginger and the Virginia Tulip tree, and a very tall (50 m, 164 ft) Norfolk pine. The gardens are considered one of the most important examples of English landscape architecture outside of the British Isles and one of the most beautiful creations of the Portuguese Romantic period.

The Palace

Reached at the end of a long, wide path, the entrance to the palace is through the southern tower. The building is perfectly symmetrical, referencing early Islamic architecture, with a large rotunda on either end and a large domed atrium in the center. The stone arches

reflect Gothic style. The main gallery extends the length of the building, providing a delightful visual rhythm as you walk through. Its lacey, open-work arches are supported by rose marble columns. In the center is the main, multi-leveled dome. Stairs lead up to the second level.

The northern tower is the location of the music room, which benefits from outstanding acoustics. This was also the Noble Hall, the main room for reception and socialization during the stays of the Cook family.

Don't miss the the views from the verandas. The lawn of the palace was the first laid lawn in Portugal, and the wide path leads down to the botanical gardens.

Across the road from the ticket office is a parking area and the beginning of a network of trails. These lead past two small lakes. The romantic Tapada de Monserrate woodland is a delightful place to spend a few

hours. Bring a picnic and enjoy the carefully contrived setting.

Getting There/Other Information

The palace is 3.5 km (2 mi) from the historic center of Sintra. Scotturb bus 435 and the red-line CitySightSeeing buses go to Monserrate. The ticket office is near the bus stop and a small parking area. If you haven't already purchased it online, you can purchase a downloadable audiovisual guide as well as tickets at this office. Monserrate is usually not as busy as Pena Palace or the Moorish Castle.

After purchasing your ticket, follow a wide path, passing through an Indian-style arch, before reaching the palace itself. Depending on the path you choose, you may pass the false cromlech or dolmen attributed to William Beckford.

Alternatively, you can opt to wander trails leading up and down through the gardens, and eventually end up at the palace. There is a cafeteria and WC conveniently located near the Boulder House, between the ticket office and the palace. If visiting the gift shop in the palace is important, check the opening and closing hours; it may be closed during lunchtime.

Monserrate
Palace

https://www.parquesdesintra.pt/pt/parques-monumentos/parque-e-palacio-de-monserrate/

Convento dos Capuchos/Capuchos Convent

"As I followed the path leading to the Capuchos Convent, I could feel myself slowing down inside and become more peaceful. I was surrounded by nature, but there was more going on than that. This a place of stillness. Not a dead, lifeless kind of stillness but a full kind of stillness, like a bird, cocking its head, listening for something. Like a friar deep in meditation. Like a smooth-surfaced pond before a raindrop strikes." — Elyn

Background

The Capuchos Convent*, also known as the Cork Convent or the Convent of the Holy Cross of the Sintra Hills, was built in 1560. It is remarkable for its utilitarian austerity and its isolation in nature. St. Francis of Assisi (1181–1226) was the founder of the Order of Friars Minor, also known as the Franciscans. St. Francis is the patron saint of ecology and of animals because he loved all creatures equally.

The Order of Friars Minor Capuchins, named for their brown robes with distinctive pointed hoods (capuchins), began as a Franciscan reform order in 1525, dedicated to living lives of strict observance, poverty, extreme simplicity, and complete submission to the spiritual life. The central belief was that by completely leaving behind worldly life, its pleasures, and even its so-called necessities, one could achieve true spiritual perfection.

The Capuchos Convent was constructed by Alvaro de Castro, Counsellor of State to Dom Sebastião and Chancellor of the Exchequer. His father, João de Castro, the fourth viceroy of India, had been charged by Dom João III to build the convent, but he had died before he could do so, leaving the project to his son to fulfill. We don't know who helped him with the unique construction, but parts of the design conform to the 17th-century Estatutos da Província de Santa Maria da Arrábida, which outlines strict rules for the construction of Capuchos convents in the province.

Legend states that Dom João III was hunting in this part of the Sintra Mountain on a hot summer's day, and, exhausted, he sought shade among the granite boulders. Or maybe it was João de Castro himself who fell asleep after chasing a deer. At any rate, one of them fell asleep and dreamt of angels worshipping a holy cross on top of the rock beneath which he was resting.

If it was the king, once he awoke he told the de Castro family, which owned the land, to build a convent* there for the Franciscans, and that it should be dedicated to the holy cross—just as he had seen in his dream. If it was João de Castro, he vowed to fulfill his dream.

The biblical Jacob also had a dream as he slept with his head resting on a rock. What is it about rocks (especially granite ones) that contributes to visionary dreams? We know that granite usually contains quartz. Since ancient times, quartz has been thought to have magical qualities and is associated with healing, restoring inner harmony, and to spiritual growth. And we now know that granite is mildly radioactive (see p. 27). The presence of large amounts of granite can lead to slight shifts in consciousness, which could be highly desirable for a group of devout friars seeking to deepen their spiritual practices. Perhaps that's why the convent is not only situated among the granite boulders but also in them and on top of them.

The small, austere, multi-level convent is built of stone, wood, tile, and cork. It is nestled in the forest, far from the distractions of worldly life, and is constructed within a field of boulders. The original community was composed of eight friars. The convent is notable for the way it melds with the boulders around it, as well as for the small size of its cells and the ubiquitous use of local cork. Cork is an excellent insulator and acoustical isolator, as well as being a natural product that was easily available. Large slabs of cork were utilized on the ceilings, doors, doorframes, windows, walls, and benches—and, occasionally, as a minimalist mattress for the monks.

The doorways to the cells are quite narrow and low, approximately 120 cm (47 in) high, and the rooms themselves are miniscule. The low doorway is usually described as a reminder of humility, since the friars would have had to kneel to enter their bedrooms. That may be true, but the miniature doorway and tiny cell would also create a sense of intimacy and, perhaps, produce the sense of entering into a protective womb. In addition, smaller insulated spaces would be easier to keep warm than larger ones.

Filipe I of Portugal (Philip II of Spain) visited the convent in 1581 and declared, "In all of my kingdom, there are two things that are much to my pleasure: the Escorial, for being so rich, and the Convent of the Holy Cross, for being so poor."

Unlike the exuberantly romantic buildings and parks scattered across the Monte da Lua, the Capuchos Convent humbly coexists with the surrounding granite boulders rather than imposing itself upon them. In fact, the friars considered the giant boulders "divine constructions." The surrounding woodland was left intact, representing today one of the most notable remaining examples of Sintra's native forest.

One memorable friar was Brother Honório, one of the original eight to live in the convent. Legend says he spent the final decades of his life in a cave in the convent's grounds, living off of bread and water, after

having succumbed to temptation. Lord Byron^ was so taken with Honório's story that he mentions it in his epic poem *Childe Harold's Pilgrimage*: "Deep in yon cave Honorius long did dwell/In hope to merit heaven, by making earth a hell."

But maybe Lord Byron misinterpreted Friar Honório's life, and he retired to the isolated shelter of the boulders so that he could enter more deeply into meditative practice. After all, the plaque next to the cave states that "he was most diligent in his teaching, to those he thought capable, spiritual exercises and mental prayer." Despite his asceticism, he was over 100 years old when he died in 1596.

Elyn visited the stone shelter of Brother Honório and wondered: Did he live out his final years consumed with guilt and penitance, or was he in a state of religious ecstasy and spiritual delight? After reading the plaque near his grotto, she votes for the latter.

After the 1834 dissolution of the monasteries, the convent and its lands were abandoned. They were acquired by the 2nd Count of Penamacor, a descendent of João de Castro, who sold it in 1873 to Sir Francis Cook, the wealthy British businessman and art collector who turned Monserrate palace and park into the Romantic confection it is today. It is interesting to compare his and Dom Fernando II's 19th-century romanticization of nature to the integral coexistence with nature embodied by the Capuchos Convent and its friars.

The State acquired the monument in 1949, at which point it was in a sad state of degradation. It has been part of the Sintra UNESCO World Heritage Site since 1995, and in 2000, management was given to Parques de Sintra. A major refurbishment and renewal project began in 2013.

What to Explore

Well-placed signage leads you to the convent and gardens. A five-minute stroll down the path from the tourist office will lead you to the Courtyard of the Crosses, representing the three crosses at Golgotha— the center standing for the crucified Christ, the two others for the two men crucified with him. Two paths

border the central cross and symbolize the freedom to choose one's way. This is where pilgrims would first arrive at the convent, seeking spiritual comfort or physical assistance and healing.

At the end of the courtyard are two large granite boulders; entrance is through a gate between them. You pass through it and up a set of stairs to a cross on top of moss-covered rocks. You have now entered a sacred space: the Fountain Courtyard, where pilgrims

would be received and offered fresh drinking water and, perhaps, a snack. You are still in the public area of the convent but are no longer in the mundane world.

At the end of the Fountain Courtyard is the Porch and a doorway with a skull and cross-bones over it. This is the Door

of Death, symbolizing renunciation of the world. The door to the left leads into the convent church and the rest of the building.

Detailed signposts guide you through the multi-level convent, from the church at the entrance to the most private space where the monks had their cramped cells; the refectory, where a stone slab served as a table for the friars as they ate their single, daily,

almost always (except twice a year) vegetarian meal; the kitchen; the infirmary; the washroom and latrine; and so on. Narrow corridors and narrow, uneven stairs, built over the different levels of bedrock and boulders, lead upward to the library and the highest room, which may have been a guestroom. Then the itinerary descends, and you can exit to the cloisters, an open-air patio, with the Hermitage of Our Lord in Gethsemane at one end.

Take time to experience the contrast between the dark, cramped spaces of the convent and the light, open exterior. Paths lead into the surrounding woodlands. This portion of the forest is known as Mata Relíquia or Relic Woodland, consisting of the original native forest (plus a few imported species). It is filled with old oaks, cork oaks (whose bark was used in the

convent), protected holly trees, strawberry trees, sweet chestnuts, hazel trees, and many other botanical specimens.

A short walk down the rocky path and uneven stairs to the left of the hermitage will take you to the cave of Friar Honório. According to legend, Friar Honório chose this covered slit between boulders as his place of hermetic retreat. The space is so small, one wonders how he could sleep there. The view of the Atlantic is exceptional, so perhaps he spent most of his time in meditation and prayer, sitting not in but on top of his so-called grotto.

There are other places to explore (consult the map), including the gardens and a picnic area. The vegetable gardens provided produce for the friars

and were also a place to commune with nature. The garden house has been converted into a WC and multi-purpose space. If you are particularly interested in local flora, the downloadable map highlights their locations. Powerful places abound in the surrounding woodlands.

Make this journey a pilgrimage rather than a tourist excursion. Begin by moving into stillness. Perhaps use the BLESSING practice on p. 10. Remember: you are venturing into what is still a sacred place. Even though the friars no longer live here, the presence of their prayers and devotion remains. Once you are centered and present, you are more likely to notice the shifts of energy that occur.

Getting There/Other Information

Be sure to wear walking shoes with good tread. The stairs within the convent are narrow and uneven, and the paths through the forest can be rocky and the steps slippery.

The Capuchos Convent is 7 km (4.3 mi) west of Sintra, on a steep slope of the Monte da Lua, a 20–25 minute drive because the route is so circuitous. The

CitySightSeeing hop-on hop-off red-line bus stops there on its return from Cabo da Roca. Another way to get there is by private car or taxi. We have been quoted prices ranging from 45€ to 100€ for the round-trip journey from downtown Sintra, including an hour of waiting at the convent. We suggest you check with different local tour guides/limo services. It's possible to take a Bolt or Uber to the convent, but it may be difficult to get a Bolt or Uber to take you back.

Capuchos Convent is somewhat less accessible and therefore not as busy as the other Sintra tourist attractions. You can buy tickets and a downloadable audiovisual guide online or at the small ticket office at the entrance. No print brochures or guidebooks are available, but you can download the site map using the QR code on the signpost next to the ticket office or by using the link below. If you don't have wifi service at the ticket office, use the free guest wifi. The coffee shop and gift shop are currently (2022) closed. There is a WC and a vending machine in the repurposed garden house.

Capuchos Convent

https://www.parquesdesintra.pt/en/parks-monuments/convent-of-the-capuchos/

Hiking trails from the convent parking lot lead to the Tholos do Monge and the Fairy Forest (see p. 161).

GPS: 38°46'58.48"N, 9°26'8.86"W

Cabo da Roca

"The wind howled, the sea heaved against the near-vertical cliffs, and the sun set with a sizzle into the ocean. I was standing, or trying to, at the most western point of the entire Eurasian land mass. I fancied I could feel the immense weight of that mass of land pushing against me, pushing me toward the white-capped waters far below. What a contrast with the green-topped Cliffs of Moher in County Clare, Ireland. Standing on their grassy heights, I had felt lulled by the rhythmic repetition of dark stone meeting foaming tide. They felt serene and timeless. This—this just felt fierce. Fierce and awesome." —Elyn

Background

Located at latitude 38º 47′north and longitude 9º 30′west, this wild and rugged promontory is the westernmost edge of the ancient eruptive Serra da Sintra, the Monte da Lua, the Mountain of the Moon. This is the place where the mountain has been worn down over millennia, where it tumbles into and under the sea. But it is more than that: Cabo da Roca is the most western spot not just of continental Europe but of the entire Eurasian land mass. It is *finisterra*, the end of the earth, where the sun sets into the sea.

The Romans called Cabo da Roca *Promontorium Magnum*. Later it was known as the Rock of Lisbon. The nearby, ruined 17th-century fort once guarded the entrance to Lisbon Harbor and played an important role during the Peninsular Wars (1809–1814). This is definitely a powerful place, geologically, geographically, and politically.

Cabo da Roca is located within the Sintra-Cascais Natural Park. It is crowned with a towering, square lighthouse topped with a circular cupola. The lighthouse stands on a rugged promontory a short distance from the cliff edge and is surrounded by a low building. A walking trail leads along the cliff, with a protective wooden parapet between you and the sea.

Cabo da Roca Lighthouse is the third oldest still in operation on the Portuguese coast. It began functioning in 1772 and was the first purpose-built lighthouse in Portugal. Its base is 165 m

(541 ft) above sea level, and it is 22 m (72 ft) high. Through the centuries, the lighthouse has undergone modernization and optimization to improve its functioning. At one point, the lighthouse was powered by olive oil, then petroleum, and later diesel fuel. It is currently automated and runs on electricity.

Below the 100-meter (328 ft) high cliffs are sandy beaches and huge, free-standing boulders called sea stacks*, against which the waves crash. The cliffs are

predominantly granite and syenite*. In recent decades, the surrounding arable land has been overrun with an invasive ground cover, which has supplanted a variety of native species. Owls, peregrine falcons, red-legged partridges, blackbirds, cormorants, Dartford warblers, stonechats, crested larks, and other marine and migratory birds find shelter along the cliffs, much to the delight of visiting birdwatchers.

Cabo da Roca was once believed to be the edge of the world. Remote and untamed, the dramatic landscape still draws people to ooh and ahh at its raw beauty and undeniable power. There is nothing here, nothing except the lighthouse, a café and gift shop, a small tourist office, and a parking lot. Nothing else but the wind, the sea, and the farthest west bit of land in Eurasia.

Well, there is one thing more. At the edge of the cliff is a large rock monument topped with a tall crucifix. An explanatory plaque on the monument's side includes a quote from Luís Vaz de Camões^, Portugal's greatest poet. Camões declared in his epic, *The Lusiads*, that

Cabo is the "crown of Europe's head," the place where "land ends and sea begins." The plaque also lists the longitude, latitude, and altitude of the location. It is a favorite spot for selfies.

We have often seen ancient standing stones "Christianized" by having a crucifix carved into them. Is this monument an attempt to "Christianize" this powerful place? It makes us wonder what pagan rituals were conducted here long ago. Perhaps during the spring and autumn equinoxes*, special ceremonies were held here in recognition of these important turning points of the year, visibly marked as the sun set into the ocean.

Legends

A kilometer north of Cabo da Roca lighthouse is Praia da Ursa, the Beach of the Bear. Its name comes from a sharply pointed sea stack that looks somewhat like a bear holding a cub and looking at the sky. The legend goes that at the end of the last Ice Age, the gods (whoever they were at that time) ordered a mother bear to migrate north with her cubs, but she refused. The gods were trying to protect the bear and her cubs because, all-knowing as they were, they knew that the ice covering Sintra Mountain would start to melt and put the bear and her cubs at risk. But the bear wanted to stay at Cabo because that's where she was born. Angry at her stubborness, the gods turned her and her cubs into rocks, which are still visible today.

Praia da Ursa is not easy to reach, but there is a well-worn, although sometimes dangerous, footpath that leads down the cliff. Once on the beach, beware of falling rocks. Praia da Ursa is wild, unspoiled, and the most western beach in continental Europe.

Here's another legend. If you turn away from the sea and look back to the Serra de Sintra, you will see the Sanctuary of Our Lady of Peninha on the nearest hilltop. It is said that, long ago, a five-year old boy who lived in a nearby village disappeared from home. His mother raised the alarm, and anxious villagers set out to find the child. They went to the cliff edge, wondering whether the child might have fallen, but if so, he could not have survived the 140 m (460 ft) drop. He was nowhere to be seen.

The villagers searched for eight days without success. Finally, some men noticed a hole about 200 m (650 ft) from where the child had been playing. It was about 2 m (6.5 ft) wide and 30 m (98 ft) deep. They saw the boy

lying at the bottom. He was so still, and it had taken so long to find him, that they thought he was dead. A villager descended by rope to retrieve him. He was alive! Weak, but alive.

After the boy recovered, which took almost no time at all, he told everyone what had happened. He explained that he had been running after a bird and fell into the deep hole. During his fall, a lady in a white robe caught him in mid-air and laid him gently on the bottom. The boy said she came every day and gave him carnation soup. He also said she told him not to worry, that he would soon be saved.

Clearly, this was a miracle. To whom could they attribute it? To whom else but Our Lady of Peninha, who had appeared as an apparition centuries ago at the site where her sanctuary now stands on the nearby hill. The grateful inhabitants soon made a pilgrimage to her shrine to give thanks.

An endangered plant species called *cravo-romano* (roman carnation) grows in the soil of Cabo, along with *cravo de Sintra* (Sintra carnation), also known as *Dianthus Centranus*. These edible carnations would have been easily available for the soup the Lady offered to the little boy.

Fierce winds and pounding surf, impressive views, the most western point in the Eurasian landmass, the site of at least one miracle—clearly Cabo da Roca is a powerful place.

Getting There/Other Information

Cabo da Roca is 18 km (11 mi) west of Sintra. You can drive, using the EN-247 road. The CitySightseeing hop-on hop-off red-line bus will take you out to the Cabo. (This bus route stops at Capuchos Convent on the way back from Cabo.)

You can also take Scotturb bus 403, which follows a loop from Sintra to Cascais and back. It stops at Cabo every hour—more or less—during the day and takes about 37 minutes (more or less) to arrive from Sintra. Check the schedule in advance, and don't expect the bus to arrive on time. Biking and hiking trails also lead along the cliffs, including one popular with birdwatchers that begins in Cascais.

The lighthouse is not open for visits. The gift shop offers a range of souvenirs and artisanal crafts. The cafeteria (with pay toilets) is on the lower level. The nearby tourist office provides, for a fee, a red-wax-

stamped official certificate proclaiming you have visited the most western site in Europe. If that is important for you, note that the Tourist Office is (probably) open 9.00 am to 7.30 pm (1st May–30th September) and 9.00 am to 6.30 pm (1st October–30th April); closed Christmas and New Year's Day.

Be prepared: it is often cold and very windy at the cape, so bring a warm jacket.

Cabo da Roca

https://www.parquesdesintra.pt/en/parks-monuments/cabo-da-roca-lighthouse/

GPS: 38°46'51"N, 9°30'2"W

Part III–Off the Beaten Path

This section is devoted to exploring powerful places in the Sintra municipality that are not as well known as the attractions described in Part II. Getting to these places is a bit more challenging since they are rarely accessible by hop-on hop-off buses or by an easy walk from Sintra town. We have provided instructions for getting to these sites, but we encourage you to use your smartphone/car GPS and to check online websites and bus schedules for the latest information. Guided hiking tours may be available for some of the places.

Santuário da Nossa Senhora da Peninha/Our Lady of Peninha Sanctuary and Nearby Sites

"I'm shaking, my legs quivering, as I struggle to climb the wide staircase leading up to the Sanctuary of Our Lady of Peninha. I don't like heights, but it's not just the buffeting wind blowing straight off the Atlantic to this high crag of granite boulders that terrifies me. It's something else. Maybe it's the power of the immense jagged rocks on which the chapel is built. Maybe it's the power of pilgrims' songs and prayers, reverberating in the stones through the centuries. Or maybe it's something else, like the reported apparition of the Virgin centuries ago. Suddenly a man appears out of nowhere. He asks me where he is, which is very odd, since you can't get to Peninha by accident. He sees me trembling and offers to help me up the stairs. He has no fear of heights, he tells me—he's a paraglider! I imagine him floating down from the sky on wings." —Elyn

Background

Located the middle of Sintra-Cascais Natural Park, Peninha is the most western of the peaks on the Monte da Lua, the Mountain of the Moon. *Peninha* means little crag or small rocky outcrop. At an elevation of 448 m (1470 ft), it is a remote, isolated place with extensive views and many reported miracles.

Peninha is home to a group of diverse sacred sites. On the rocky crag itself are an 18th-century chapel dedicated to the apparition of our Lady of Peninha, several pilgrimage shelters, and a 20th-century fortified mansion built by the same Carvalho Monteiro who built Quinta da Regaleira (see p. 53). Down the hill a short distance is the partly ruined Santuário de São Saturnino (Sanctuary of Saint Saturnin), built in the 16th century over a much-earlier hermitage. Hiking trails pass by the sanctuary and lead to the nearby 6,000-year-old Anta* (Dolmen*) de Adrenunes and the powerful Pedras Irmãs, the two house-size, granite Sisters Rocks. Offerings of flowers, coins, fruit, candles, and (occasionally) sacrificed birds are sometimes found alongside the trail and near the Sisters Rocks.

The Sanctuary of Our Lady of Peninha

According to legend, sometime in the 16th century, during the reign of Dom João III, the Virgin Mary ("Our Lady") appeared at that very spot to a poor, mute shepherd or (depending on the account) shepherdess from nearby Amoinhas Velhas. The shepherdess had lost one of her sheep and was searching frantically for it. Suddenly she saw Our Lady coming towards her, holding the lost sheep in her arms.

Our Lady asked the shepherdess to give her some bread, but the poor girl had none. Our Lady told her that when she arrived home, she should ask her mother for bread. The mute shepherdess tried to explain how impossible this would be, both because she could not speak and because they were so poor that they had no bread, but she promised she would try.

She returned home, called to her mother, and discovered that she could speak. A miracle had occurred! Together they searched the house and found enough bread in a chest to feed the entire hungry village. In thanksgiving for both miracles, the villagers climbed up to the place where the shepherdess had met Our Lady. They erected a statue of Her and constructed a crude altar. Soon the site of the apparition became an important place of pilgrimage, especially for sailors and their families, who prayed for their safe return.

After several unsuccessful attempts to build a chapel, the current sanctuary was completed in 1711, thanks both to the dedication of the hermit Pedro da Conceição and to Dom Pedro II, who provided financial assistance. The bright-ochre Pilgrims' Houses were built between 1751–1761 to house the caretakers and the numerous pilgrims who ventured up the remote, isolated hilltop to pray in the chapel or look out to sea for returning ships.

The interior of the chapel (now closed to the public) is a fine example of Portuguese Baroque architecture. The interior walls are covered with narrative blue-and-white tiled panels depicting the life of Our Lady, Pentecost, and the childhood of Jesus. The chapel has marble interiors, and the pulpit contains various inscriptions made by pilgrims. The Baroque altar is framed with spiral columns and decorated with a Florentine mosaic. The front of the altar features several seven-pointed stars and other symbols designating the Virgin Mary as Queen of the World and the Star of the Sea—symbols often associated with other, more ancient goddesses.

Although the chapel is usually closed, the terraces around it are always open. The view of Cabo da Roca and the surrounding countryside is impressive. On a clear day you can see up to 50 km (30 mi), to Cape Espichel in the south, Ericeira in the north, and Lisbon to the southeast.

In 1892, the 62-hectare (153–acre) Peninha complex was bought by the Count of Almedina. It was then sold to António Augusto Carvalho Monteiro. In 1918 he began to build a "mini" Pena Palace conjoined to the chapel. He died before the building was completed, and the property was sold to Dr. José Maria Ferreira Rangel de Sampaio, who wanted to finalize the project in much the same manner as Carvalho Monteiro had planned. Rangel de Sampaio also died before its completion. He left the complex to his alma mater, the Faculty of Law at the University of Coimbra. Although the chapel was now private property, pilgrimages continued to the site in the 20th century.

Why would Carvalho Monteiro choose this site to build upon? This man did not make architectural decisions lightly. Did he sense something special about this place, something he could link to the initiatic journey he had created at Quinta da Regaleira? When you visit the site, sense, see, and feel into your surroundings. Do you gain any insights into his choice of location?

In 1991, the complex was purchased by the government and placed under the management of the Institute for Nature Conservation and Forests. In 2017, Parques de Sintra took over plans to rehabilitate the sanctuary, promote nature conservation and education, and better link it to other sites on Sintra Mountain.

Although the mansion cannot be visited, it appears to have been constructed with the same underlying esoteric philosophies as Quinta da Regaleira (see p. 53). According to the esoteric writer Vitor Manuel Adrião^, the building includes numerous

Rosicrucian, Masonic, Hermetic, and alchemical symbols. "The entire building is arranged in a downward spiral.… In addition to a small staircase that leads to the terrace at the back of the hall, in another space for the living room, there is another staircase, in the middle of the entrance room, which leads to an underground quadrangular room, open to the side of a cistern whose depth is lost in the abysses of the Earth. An iron grate door, fallen and rusty, in turn provided access" (p. 278) … "to another smaller room, which had in one of its corners a kind of altar in a triangle mounted in the living rock itself" (p. 279).

Nearby Sites to Explore

Santuário de São Saturnino/Sanctuary of Saint Saturnin

Just a short distance down the hill is the ruined 16th-century Sanctuary (or Hermitage) of Saint

Saturnin. It was built over a hermitage constructed in the 12th century by Pêro Pais, officer and standard-bearer to Dom Afonso Henriques, the first king of Portugal. Evidence of a medieval necropolis has also been found, as well as a cistern built into the rock.

It's possible the site has been sacred for much, much longer. The hermitage is oriented toward the rising sun on Beltane (May 1). Luis Élye^ suggests this indicates there was a pagan temple at the site, dedicated to the god Baal, an ancient fertility god, whose feastday was celebrated on that day. The presence of cup-like libation depressions carved into the large nearby boulder adds credence to this theory.

The current building was built in the mid-16th century, expanded in the 17th century, and inhabited by monks until the dissolution of the monasteries in Portugal in 1834. It was still occupied by farmers until the 1960s, after which time it was used as a barn. Although in a bad state of disrepair, bits of interior fresco and painted crosses are still visible on the interior arches.

Although the hermitage is in ruins, it is still a sacred space. Center yourself, ask permission before you enter, perhaps use the BLESSING process (see p. 10). How does it feel inside? What do you notice? Elyn found it surprisingly quiet and peaceful, even though the interior is a shambles. She wondered if the tranquility she felt was because the hermitage provided shelter from the wind or whether something else was going on. After all, the site has been sacred for nearly a millennium—and probably for millennia.

Anta de Adrenunes/Dolmen of Adre Nunes

A completely different sacred site is the many-millennia-old Anta* (Dolmen*) de Adrenunes, reached by following the trail that leads from São Saturnino into the forest. This megalithic structure is at an elevation of 426 m (1398 ft), a little lower than the Sanctuary of Our Lady of Peninha.

Located in the midst of dense vegetation, on top of a slight rise, it was first excavated in the 19th century. Ever since then, the *anta* has been the source of much debate. Is it entirely natural, a mere happenstance of nature? Is it human-made? Was it a funerary monument, although no remains have been found?

The archaeological consensus is that the massive jumbled pile of upright granite boulders and horizontal stone slabs is only partly natural. There is clear indication of human intervention, including wedges and blocks used to help define the space, and evidence of a floor in the gallery. There is a gap in the roof, perhaps caused by shifting in the overhead stone slabs. The west-opening gallery is 5 m (16 ft) high and is oriented to the sun and moon setting into the Atlantic Ocean.

Spend time exploring the anta, walking around it and climbing on the flat roof. Center yourself, be present, and try to experience the energy of the place.

In recent years the *anta* has become a popular place to visit during solstices* and equinoxes*. Its age is difficult to determine, but it might be 6,000 years old or older. There was human habitation on the Serra de Sintra long before then.

When we visited the anta, we encountered a local shamanic guide with two companions. She told us there was an age-old tradition that visitors to the *anta* should climb on top of it and slide down into the gallery through the hole in the roof. She said this was an ancient ritual of rebirth. Elyn privately doubted that was the intent of the dolmen builders. Nonetheless, this perhaps-invented tradition demonstrates the ongoing importance of this sacred site.

The rocky crag of Peninha and the nearby forest are very powerful places. They have drawn people to them for millennia, including megalith builders, Christian hermits, at least one hermeticist/alchemist, and modern-day Afro-Brazilian and shamanic practitioners. One has to wonder how these sacred sites were originally connected and whether there is any link between the ancient goddess worshipped on the Monte da Lua (see p. 11) and the more recent apparition of Our Lady, who also reportedly appeared at Cabo da Roca to save a young child's life (see p. 127).

What to Explore

Let's start at the Sanctuary of Peninha parking lot. Once you pass through the entry gate, follow the wide cobblestone path up the hill. In the distance above, to the right, you can see the ochre-colored pilgrimage shelters. The grey building with the crenellated roofline is Carvalho Monteiro's unfinished mansion. Behind it, but not visible until you reach the top, is the small sanctuary itself, with its badly defaced, locked wooden door.

As you continue walking, the path bifurcates. To your right is the path that leads to the Pilgrims' Houses and the Sanctuary of Peninha. To your left is the path that leads to the Sanctuary (Hermitage) of Saint Saturnin.

If you continue to the Sanctuary of Peninha, you will come to steps and then a wide staircase. On one side of the staircase is granite bedrock and the foundations of the buildings; on the other is a sturdy, meter-high wall. Both the sanctuary and mansion are usually closed to the public, but the terraces are always open and the views are outstanding. From the top, on a clear day you can see the lighthouse at Cabo da Roca in the distance. Be aware that the wind blows in from thousands of miles across the ocean, and it can be quite intense.

If you want to visit the Sanctuary of San Saturnin, take the lower trail to the left instead of continuing up the rocky crag. You will see the hermitage in front of you. Just past the hermitage is a T-intersection. To the right is the signposted GR10 loop trail that will lead you into the forest to the Anta de Adrenunes. The loop is approximately 5 km (3 mi) long.

Getting There/Other Information

To reach the Sanctuary of Peninha it is necessary to go by private car, taxi, Bolt/Uber, or electric bike— or be prepared for a very long hike. If you use hired transport, make sure to make arrangements in advance to be picked up at a certain time: cellphone service can be erratic on the hilltop.

Sanctuary of Peninha GPS: 38°46'06.7"N 9°27'37.8"W

Driving yourself: It is very likely that if you follow Google Maps it will lead you in ways that are not the best. The Sanctuary is located near Malveira da

Serra, partway between Sintra and Cascais, about ½ hour from Sintra. From Sintra, head south along the N9 towards Cascais. At approximately 6 km (3.7 mi) from Sintra, turn right onto the N9-1, signposted to Malveira da Serra. Follow this road approximately 7 km (4.3 mi) until just before the village. There are switchbacks. Turn right onto Caminho dos Fetos, a narrow but paved road. The journey is a further 2.5 km (1.5 mi) along this road. After 400 m (1/4 mi) take a right at the crossroads. After 1.3 km (0.8 mi) turn right at the T-junction and continue straight on and uphill to the parking lot and gate for Peninha Sanctuary. (Directions from https://www.sintra-portugal.com/Attractions/Santuario-Peninha-Chapel-Sintra.html/)

The Anta de Adrenunes is about 1 km (5/8 mi) from a tarred road and can also be reached by following the PR10 hiking trail that passes near the Sanctuary of Peninha. It is advisable to consult a walking app for details. GPS: 38°46'41"N 9°27'52"W

Walking Apps for this Area

Walk Sintra. https://walksintra.com/pr10-peninha/

https://www.alltrails.com/parks/portugal/lisboa--6/parque-natural-de-sintra-cascais/

Another good app for this region (including Monserrat, Capuchos, etc.): www.WalkMePortugal.com

info@parquesdesintra.pt for information about the Sanctuary of Peninha.

Capela de Santa Eufémia/Saint Eufémia Chapel and Nearby Sites

"At the top of the hill is a small chapel that once was a popular pilgrimage site. Legend says that the apparition of Santa Eufémia appeared there. Proof can be seen in the supposed stone impression of her footprint, visible in the bedrock in a niche in the exterior north wall of the chapel. A curative spring is located nearby. Neolithic, Bronze-Age, and Roman remains discovered at the site are evidence of the lengthy sacredness of the place. After all, fresh water is always important, and water with healing properties even more so." —Elyn

Background

On the hillside above São Pedro de Penaferrim is a chapel dedicated to Santa Eufémia. She was a virgin martyred in Chalcedon in 307 by Diocletian. Santa Eufémia is the patroness of diseases of the body, mainly scabies, liver, and ulcerations. The miraculous power of Santa Eufémia—or at least the strength

of devotion to her—is demonstrated by the large collection of wax ex-votos* displayed in the chapel's vestry. Some of them are very old. Downhill from the chapel is a bathhouse associated with the healing spring, and uphill is a *miradouro* (overview) marked by a high cross.

The site of Santa Eufémia is considered "the cradle of Sintra." Situated near Sintra, Pena Palace, and the Moorish Castle, it is one of the oldest locales with proven human habitation on the Mountain of the Moon. It is also a place where ancient habitation and Christian sacredness co-exist. Neolithic vestiges dating back to 4000 BCE, as well as Bronze-Age and Iron-Age artifacts, have been found there. It is likely that the healing spring was known in Roman times, if not before. Roman remains dating from the 2nd century BCE to as late as the 2nd century

CE, including two column shafts that belonged to a Roman temple, attest to the long-recognized sanctity of this location.

Unfortunately, due to urban pressure and the expansion of roads in the area, the Neolithic and Roman settlements have been partially destroyed. It is thought that a section of the modern asphalt road covers the original Roman road, and the construction earthworks destroyed many vestiges of the Neolithic village.

The curative waters were mentioned in the chronicle of a crusader who accompanied troops in the conquest of Lisbon in 1147. He wrote that the waters of the nearby spring were thought to have therapeutic powers. He described "a most pure spring, whose waters, to those who drink it, they say, soothe cough and consumption; so when the natives hear someone cough, they immediately understand that it is a stranger."

The reputation of the healing waters led to the construction of the chapel sometime in the 13th century. It soon became a popular site of pilgrimage and local devotion. None of the original medieval building remains, however, because in 1876 a foreigner devoted to the saint had the chapel completely rebuilt. In later years, the chapel fell into disrepair. According to a custodian, it was rebuilt through volunteer efforts in the 1970s.

The outside of the stone chapel is white-painted plaster. There are several external buttresses. The white-

painted interior of the church is quite simple, with a single nave, a choir balcony in the west, and a raised pulpit on the north wall, accessible from an exterior

staircase. The altar is simple as well, but quite pretty with green accents on the arches. It is a pleasing, harmonious space.

A grate-covered niche at foundation-level in the exterior of the north wall of the chapel displays evidence of a miraculous event. Visible in the bedrock is the so-called footprint left by the apparition of Santa Eufémia. Inside the niche, a blue-and-white tile dated 1787 commemorates the event, although the time of the event itself is left unclear.

This would not be the first time a feminine deity has appeared on the Monte da Lua. Pena Palace was founded over a monastery built over an earlier chapel commemorating a reported apparition of the Virgin (see p. 86), and the Sanctuary of Peninha owes its origin to a similar apparition (see

p. 134). When this deity/energy form appeared on the mountain millennia ago, she was identified as the goddess of the moon and wild beasts. When the Romans arrived in Sintra, they claimed her as the goddess Cynthia or Diana. With the coming of Christianity, she became known as either a saint or the Virgin Mary.

Gary dowsed outside the church and found a fire line (a naturally occurring underground fissure or crack) that goes down the central aisle of the nave. He found a water line (a naturally occurring underground water channel) crossing the fire line at the division between the main church and the apse* at the back. Since he was dowsing outside the building, he could not determine if the crossing was near or directly under the altar.

Gary often finds a fire line crossing a water line near the altar in churches. In the Middle Ages, many churches were intentionally located over these underground currents to enhance the energy of the church. Gary dowsed another water line going into the church on the north, where the external standing pipe (now dry) is located. This line went through the font and angled off to the northwest corner of the church near the entrance.

East of the chapel is a humble stone

building, the Casa dos Romeiros (Pilgrims´ House), which was built or rebuilt in the 19th century. The large churchyard that surrounds the chapel was

transformed at some point into a leisure area with a tribune, bandstand, and picnic area. The size of the leisure area indicates that popular devotion to Santa Eufémia was at some point much greater than today. There are 20th-century reports that pilgrims made an annual pilgrimage from as far away as Lisbon. Currently there are two large *romarías* (day-pilgrimages with food, dancing, and celebration) to the chapel, one on May 1 and one on September 16 (Santa Eufémia's saint's day).

The path behind the chapel leads up through an atmospheric, boulder-strewn forest to the high cross and overlook. The Miradouro de Santa Eufémia was constructed in 1976. It is 470 m (1542 ft) high, commanding an exceptional view of the surrounding region. You can see Pena Palace through the woods, and you can see Lisbon to the southeast, Mafra to the north, and the ocean to the west.

As you walk up the path to the overview, notice the changes in energy. Elyn felt a distinct shift as she walked between two large trees near the beginning of the trail. Gary felt a great deal of energy coming off the large boulders further up the trail to the right. Changes in energy ("energy gateways") often occur around sacred sites, sometimes forming concentric circles.

The healing waters spring from the earth at the Casa dos Banhos/Bathhouse, 220 m (722 ft) down the road from the chapel. In 1438 the Archbishop of Viseu went to the baths in search of a cure for his leprosy*. In 1738 the medieval fountain at that location was reconstructed into a bathhouse, with additional reforms in 1845. The small structure is built into the hillside, with one side open to the path. A faucet drips water into a small basin. The room on the right is accessed through a doorway that opens onto a small

space with a barrel vault. Inside is a rectangular bathing tank. The Bathhouse was opened to the public in April 2013, although it is now locked, and the building is covered with a great deal of leafy vegetation.

Getting There/Other Information

To get to the chapel and overlook: First, you need to get to São Pedro de Penaferrim. From Sintra, take a taxi, Bolt, tuk-tuk, or bus. Or walk. The chapel is a long, steep walk of approximately 4 km (2.5 mi) from Sintra.

If you take Scotturb bus 417, 418, or 433 to the zone "Chão de Meninos" in São Pedro, ring the bell to be let off at the bus stop just after the bakery/café Casa do Preto (you will see the large white building on the right), then walk a little further down the road and turn right on the Rua 1° de Dezembro. Then turn right on Rua Tude de Sousa, and turn left onto Rua Marquês Viana, just before the big outdoor marketplace/public parking area at Largo D. Fernando II. (This big market, including clothes and antiques, is held there every 2nd and 4th Sunday of the month.)

A small road sign at the corner indicates the turn to the sanctuary and *miradouro*. Rua Marquês Viana becomes Calçada José Joaquim Gonçalves, which becomes Rua da Santa Eufémia as it winds up the hill. There is a parking lot just below the church.

Be aware that some of the GPS driving instructions appear to have a glitch in them. If your taxi/Bolt has taken you into São Pedro but then starts to go downhill, it is going the wrong way. The road you want to take goes up the hill, not down.

The chapel is only open once a week, possibly on Sunday afternoon at 3 pm for an hour or two.

Address: Miradouro and Chapel of Santa Eufémia da Serra: Largo da Capela de Santa Eufémia, Rua de Santa Eufémia.

GPS: 38°47'12.3"N, 9°23'06.75"W

To get to the Bathhouse: After you arrive in the parking lot at the Church of Santa Eufémia, walk to the picnic area in front of the church. As you face the church, you will see the road to the Banhos just after the stone seating area on your left. Follow the asphalt road down the hill. Soon you will pass a large building on the right. Continue around the corner. On your left you will see a sign pointing to a trail in the forest that goes to the Bathhouse and also to Pena Palace. There is also an explanatory plaque. The Bathhouse is just below the level of the road. The

Bathhouse is locked, and when we visited it in 2022 it was deteriorating, but you can look inside. The entrance to Pena Palace is about 10 minutes away on a sometimes-slippery trail.

Nearby Sites to Explore

São Pedro de Penaferrim has several other sacred sites to visit that are easily reached on foot once you are in the town. Large, beige-colored plaques are scattered throughout town to direct you to different locations on "The Roteiro Medieval de S. Pedro/Medieval Tour of S. Pedro." These sites include the Hermitage/Chapel of Santa Eufémia, the Banhos, the Fonte de São Pedro/St. Peter's Fountain, the Capela de São Lázaro/St. Lazarus Chapel, and the Igreja de São Pedro de Penaferrim/St. Peter's Church.

The Chapel of St. Lazarus (usually closed) dates back to the late 15th century. It was built next to a hospital and related leprosery, which may date back to the 14th century or before. In the late 15th century, Dona Leonor and Dom João II had the Chapel of St. Lazarus built (or rebuilt) to give religious assistance to

the lepers of the leprosery. There are two barred side windows through which the lepers could attend mass (at a distance). You can see the symbols in the chapel of the shrimp (Dona Leonor) and the pelican (Dom João II).

The chapel is located on Rua Serpa Pinto 17, São Pedro de Sintra, tel. (+351) 219 231 157. GPS: 38°47'29.8"N, 9°22'51.8"W.

St. Peter's Fountain provided the water for the leprosery during the Middle Ages. Its water continued to be used for private and commercial purposes in the 20th century. In 2022, the fountain had become neglected, its shallow basin covered with greenery. From N375, take Rua Serpa Pinto to the Caminho da Fonte de São Pedro to the end; the fountain is on the left.

St. Peter's Church was begun in the 14th century and replaced the earlier church of São Pedro de Canaferrim, located at the Moorish Castle (see p. 93), when people moved down the hillside toward Sintra.

Perhaps because of damage resulting from the 1531 earthquake, reconstruction was undertaken in 1565. Further changes were made over the centuries to the single-nave church, changing its style to Manueline and Baroque.

The church is built directly on the bedrock, and Elyn felt very grounded and peaceful inside. As you visit different sacred sites and powerful places, sense how you feel. For example, are you relaxed in one location? Do you feel energized or uncomfortable in another?

The interior walls are covered with fine 18th–century blue-and-white tile panels showing the life of St. Peter. It's possible the stone sculpture of Saint Peter high on

the north wall is from the 12th century. The 14th century sculpture of Saint Catherine of Alexandria was originally at St Peter's Church at the Moorish Castle. It is quite fine, and the saint's presence may be a reference to the Knights Templar*, who considered her one of their patrons. A stone Catherine's Wheel (referring to her method of martyrdom) over the altar may be another such reference.

Gary dowsed a water line down the central aisle and a fire line crossing at the altar. Our guide was very interested in the process. She wondered if an underground water channel was the reason the west end of the north wall in the entryway to the sacristy was always damp. She explained that they had just repainted it, but a month later the paint had bubbled up again. Gary dowsed a water line under the wall, which confirmed her suspicions.

Address: Largo do Adro da Igreja 6A, 2710-507 Sintra. Telephone (+351) 219 230 844

https://www.gpsmycity.com/attractions/st-peter-church-(igreja-da-sao-pedro)-43217.html/

Check open hours online at http://www.paroquias-sintra.pt/unidade-pastoral-de-sintra/penaferrim/

Market in São Pedro: https://uniaodasfrequesias-sintra.pt/feiradesaopedro/

Tholos do Monge/Monk's Tomb and the Fairy Forest

"I had no expectations, or, rather, I had very low expectations. The roofless megalithic site had been neglected for decades, and I had seen recent photos (April 2022) showing that it was now in a state of even worse disrepair. But I wanted to see it, so I hiked a mile uphill through the so-called Fairy Forest. Just as I suspected, the tholos was a jumbled-up mess, partially covered with white and black plastic tarps. Then I noticed something else. The top of the large upright stone in the chamber was surrounded by a faint halo, as were two large horizontal slabs along the edge. I 'centered' myself and felt into the space. It was full of bright, expansive energy, so powerful that it almost took my breath away." —Elyn

Background

Originally discovered in 1878, the Tholos* do Monge is an approximately 4,500-year-old megalithic structure, located at the third-highest elevation (491 m/1610 ft) on the Serra de Sintra, the Monte da Lua. It is in a dominant position on the ridge line of the mountain. The tholos is near the Capuchos Convent, hence its name, "Monk's Tomb," although no monks were buried there.

The tholos is in a moody, evocative woodland known as the Fairy or Druid Forest. It is marked by a very tall geodetic triangulation monument, which makes

it easy to find. Standing beside the tholos, you have an exceptional view to the south to the ocean and Cascais, and (through the trees) to the west to Cabo da Roca.

The semi-subterranean tholos was built between 2500 and 1500 BCE and reused in the Bronze Age (between 1800 and 800 BCE). The tomb faces north; that is, it opens to the south (200° SSW). It may well have been one of the sacred places on the Monte da Lua that were still remembered, and possibly still in use, when the Romans arrived. The limestone lunations* found nearby attest to the important cult* of the Goddess of the Moon. The tholos may have been a place of burial, a place of worship, or both. Located on one of the highest points on the Sacred Mountain, it served for millennia as an important meeting place—and continues to do so today.

The tholos was built to take advantage of a naturally occurring depression in the granite bedrock, which was then artificially shaped and covered with blocks of the same stone. Originally, the tholos was composed of an atrium, a passage, and a circular chamber, covered with a false dome. In the last 100 years, the tholos has been so badly damaged that it is hard to make out the details of the construction.

The atrium was irregular in plan, 6.5 m (21 ft) in length and 6 m (19.5 ft) wide. A rectangular corridor about 1 m (3 ft) in length connected it to the circular chamber. This burial (or ceremonial?) chamber has a diameter of 4.5 m (15 ft). The walls, built of different-sized slabs, were approximately 2 m (6.5 ft) high and were covered with a false dome, which could have

included a skylight made with perishable materials. A skylight in a burial chamber? Perhaps it wasn't.

During the initial excavations, a number of artifacts from different epochs were found, including flints, arrowheads, pottery fragments, vases, and an ochre cone.

Gary dowsed a fire line going through the length of the tholos. It crossed a water line that went through the central chamber. He often finds a similar pattern in medieval churches.

About 100 m (328 ft) from the tholos is an atmospheric clearing in the Fairy/Druid Forest, and at one side of the clearing is the Painted Rock. This is a 3 m (10 ft) high, vertically split, granite boulder with a circular design painted on the front face, near the top. The legend goes that this was a place where the Druids (the religious specialists of the Celts) worshipped. According to the story, where the Painted Rock stands there was once a special, magical tree….

There are several problems with the legend. The vine-draped boulder has stood where it is for a very long time, long before anyone could have seen a tree growing there. Nor is it clear who painted the design (a Sanskrit Om in a circle) on the rock, or when. The clearing in the forest does appear to be quite old, however, and a tree stump is visible near the Painted Rock, along with some logs to sit upon.

"As we walked up the forestry trail, the tall eucalyptus trees swayed in the wind, rubbing their flexible trunks against each other and moaning. I could imagine how evocative a journey in the forest would be on a moonlit night. It's not surprising that people come here to do rituals under the new and full moons." — Elyn

Druids often worshipped in sacred groves in the forest, so perhaps there is truth hidden in the story. The nearby tholos was reused during the Bronze Age, the time when the Druids might, indeed, have been conducting ceremonies in the clearing. It is possible that the legend is a faint memory not of a magical tree but of the nearby, magical tholos. Or perhaps it is a coded reference to the fact that the Druids' veneration of nature was supplanted (cut down, like the magical tree) by Christianity.

Elyn felt a lot of energy near the Painted Rock. It was heavy energy and almost pushed her away. She said it was not negative, just very strong.

Regardless of the truth of the Painted Rock legend, the clearing has a special energy. The forested slopes of the Monte da Lua conceal a number of sacred sites and places of power. Given the evocative atmosphere

of the Sacred Mountain, it is not surprising that people still do rituals and leave offerings in the woods. We saw one such offering at the base of a tree at the crossroads near the beginning of the forestry road.

Getting There/Other Information

The Tholos do Monge and Painted Rock in the Fairy Forest can be reached via several hiking trails. There are also organized hikes through the Fairy Forest that can be discovered by doing a Google search.

WalkSintra app offers a 4 km (2.5 mi) loop trail starting at the Capuchos Convent parking lot. It includes 252 m (827 ft) of ascent/descent. See p. 120 for how to get to the Capuchos Convent. https://walksintra.com/the-fairy-forest-trail/

You can also begin your hike at the unpaved forestry road at the junction just before the turn-off to the convent. The forestry road goes uphill (sometimes steeply, other times not as steeply) for about a mile, passing by a large monument, the Memorial dos Soldados, dedicated to the firefighters killed during the 1966 Sintra mountain forest fire. As you approach the top of the serra*, you will see a PR11 trail sign on the right that will take you into the Fairy Forest to the Painted Rock. If you stay on the forestry road, you will come to a T-intersection. In front of you is a very tall geodetic triangulation marker. The PR6/ PR11 trail sign on the left points to the Tholos do Monge located just behind the monument. If you follow the dirt road to the right instead of going to the tholos,

you would eventually reach the Sanctuary of Peninha (see p. 132).

How long will it take you to reach the tholos? That all depends. It took Elyn almost an hour to reach the tholos via the forestry road. She is a slow walker uphill. It took about 25 minutes to return on the same road.

Alltrails provides a longer hiking loop. It is listed as a moderately challenging route: 9.7 km (6 mi), elevation gain 479 m (1571 ft). This circular route passes by the Mula River Dam, Capuchos Convent, Memorial of the Soldiers, and Yellow Stone. https://www.alltrails. com/trail/portugal/lisboa--6/tholos-do-monge-pedra-amarela-e-barragem-do-rio-da-mula/

GPS: 38°46'27.2064"N, 9°26'28.896"W

Museu Arqueológico de São Miguel de Odrinhas/ Archaeology Museum of Saint Michael of Odrinhas and Barreira Megalithic Complex

"We don't usually think of an archeology museum as a powerful place, but this museum is an exception because of its location. It is next to a Roman villa, a 12th-century church, and a medieval cemetery. Visible on a nearby hill is the Barreira Megalithic Complex. At least some of the stones appear to have been manipulated by humans. These varied constructions demonstrate the ongoing attraction of ancient sacred sites to later inhabitants." —Elyn

Background

For thousands of years, Sintra has been home to diverse communities of various origins and cultural traditions. Paleolithic, Neolithic, Bronze Age, Iron Age, Roman, Moorish, Christian—many different people have settled in the region and left behind material remains. Local farmers and villagers have collected them, and archaeologists have dug for them. The area around São Miguel de Odrinhas is an excellent example of "the power of place" that draws people to re-use the same location over millennia.

The Archaeology Museum of San Miguel de Odrinhas (MASMO)

The Archaeology Museum of San Miguel de Odrinhas (MASMO) explores the history of the region for over 2,000 years, beginning with the 1st century BCE. The highlight is the largest Portuguese collection of Roman epigraphic* stones.

The museum traces its origins to the 16th century, when several local scholars, including Francisco de Holanda, collected a number of Roman artifacts from the area and placed them together near the parish church of São Miguel. In 1955, the Sintra Town Council constructed a small museum at the site to bring together the antiquities already discovered and those that would be discovered in future archaeological excavations. In the 1990s, construction began on the spacious, modern museum, which opened in 1999.

The lapidary collection comprises more than 400 pieces. In addition, there are thousands of coins, ceramics, metallic objects, osteological finds, and more. The exhibits are arranged in two sections: the Epigraphy Section ("The Book of Stone"), spanning 2,000 years from the Etruscan to the Modern Age; and the Archaeology Section, which includes a few million artifacts from the Sintra region, dating from the middle Paleolithic to the 18th century. In this section are displayed objects discovered during excavations at Alto da Vigia (see p. 179).

The Epigraphy Section is arranged as a journey through "The Book of Stone." The different kinds of stone artifacts are treated as chapters or pages in the book. Chapters include "The Etruscan Crypt" (with three Etruscan tombs purchased as garden ornaments in the 1850s by the then-owner of Monserrate Palace), "The Roman Basilica" (with dozens of monuments attesting to Roman presence), "The Visigothic Church" (containing carved lintels), "Cronos Devorator" (filled with Roman tombstones that were re-used for other purposes), "The Medieval Necropolis" (sepulcher lids and headstones ranging from the 12th to 16th century, some bearing what looks like a Templar cross on one side), and "The Lapidary Room" (which explores the scientific study of epigraphs). There is also "The Otium Fecundum," a room and patio that evoke Moorish Iberia and "fruitful leisure," and "The Fines" (the end of the museum, marked by a collection of boundary stones).

The Archaeology Section is dedicated to numerous Sintra-region discoveries that range from the Middle Paleolithic Age to the 18th century. Pieces from the Neolithic, Chalcolithic, and Roman periods deserve special mention. There is an extensive explanation of the finds at Alto da Vigia.

The museum also has a large auditorium, a café (which may or may not be open), and a research library of 80,000 volumes that is open to the public. Historic books in the collection date from the 16th- to mid-19th centuries.

Conjunto Megalítico de Barreira/Barreira Megalithic Complex

The Barreira Megalithic Complex is located on top of a small, wooded hill within sight of the museum. The view in all directions is impressive. This is a confusing site, filled with numerous large moss- and lichen-covered stones, some upright, some half-buried.

The path enters the megalithic site between two moss-covered standing stones. This feels like an energetic gateway. Can you feel the energy shift?

Archaeologists think the complex includes approximately 24 menhirs (standing stones) of different shapes and sizes, ranging from 1 m (3 ft) to 4 m (13 ft) tall. The shorter ones are cylindrical or flat-topped, and the tallest ones are slim and somewhat pointed.

Although most of the site seems to be natural, archaeologists speculate that the complex was

originally a dolmen* or a cromlech (stone circle), but a number of stones have been removed, including a tall central menhir, making its original form hard to reconstruct. Some of the remaining limestone megaliths appear to have man-made dimples (depressions) in them, which may represent pairs of eyes. Or they may be indicative of the deterioration of the stone surface.

Despite the disarray, the place is powerful—and that isn't because the rocks are granite. They are limestone. One 2.5 m (8 ft) high upright stone in the north part of the complex drew us to it. Its rough sides pockmarked from deterioration, it still has a compelling presence.

The site is on private land and has been sadly disturbed. Since 1961, when it was first identified as a megalithic complex, some of the stones, including the central menhir, have been removed.

What to Explore

A visit to the museum (guided visits are available in English with advance request) begins with exploring the nearby surroundings. The remains of the early 4th-century Roman villa of São Miguel de Odrinhas are next to the museum. For several centuries the exact nature of the still-visible, circular stone chamber has been debated. It might be the remains of the arched apse* of a Roman temple, a Paleo-Christian baptistery, or a basilica. Or it might be the *exedra* or main room of the Roman villa. A lovely 4th-century mosaic floor has been uncovered next to the chamber.

The 12th-century parish church of São Miguel is still in use. It was built over the Roman villa by Dom Afonso Henriques, the first king of Portugal. It was probably constructed in part from stones from the ruined villa. The church was heavily damaged in the 1755 Lisbon earthquake and rebuilt.

A medieval cemetery was discovered beside the church and has been partially excavated. Some of the headstones can still be seen *in situ;* others are on display in the museum. Some of the rounded headstones have a cross engraved on one side and, on the other side, the Seal of Solomon, a six-pointed star surrounded by a circle. Some engraved stars are five-pointed, not six. Our guide (Patricia) explained that the markings on

the tombstones served a double purpose: the cross for good luck, the star to repel evil.

Luis Élye[^] told us that the graveyard might well be a Templar cemetery. There are documents that indicate that the land was given to Gualdim Pais, Grand Master of the Templars. That would explain the numerous Templar crosses on the headstones, as well as the pentangles and Seals of Solomon.

The earliest medieval headstones have symbols but no names, perhaps

because most of the people were illiterate. The museum room called "The Medieval Necropolis" displays a number of these stones, supposedly in chronological order, and carved with varied degrees of skill and complexity of design.

If you are interested in visiting a powerful place instead of seeing pieces in a museum, the Barreira Megalithic Complex is within easy walking distance. It is on private land but is usually accessible. A visit to the site gives you a sense of the surrounding area, its lengthy occupation, and the ongoing attraction and re-use of powerful places.

Getting There/Other Information

A car, taxi, or Bolt/Uber is advisable to reach the museum. It is approximately 12 km (7.5 mi) from Sintra. A bus service run by Mafrense departs hourly from Sintra at the Portela de Sintra terminal next to the train station. Take the Ericeira bus and alight at Barreira, near the museum and the megaliths.

https://www.mafrense.pt/

Museu Arqueológico de São Miguel de Odrinhas
Avenida Prof. Dr. D. Fernando de Almeida
São Miguel de Odrinhas

2705-739 São João das Lampas
GPS: 38°53'13.5"N, 09°21'58.6"W
Tel: (+351) 219 609 520
Tel: (+351) 219 238 608
E-mail: dbmu.masmo.geral@cm-sintra.pt
Hours: Tuesday-Saturday: 10 am to 1 pm, 2 pm to 6 pm. Closed Sunday, Monday, and holidays. The library is closed in August. It is advisable to call to be sure the museum is open.

To request a guided visit (available in English) call in advance. Tel: (+351) 219 609 520

Archeology
Museum

https://cm-sintra.pt/atualidade/cultura/museus-municipais-de-sintra/museu-arqueologico-de-sao-miguel-de-odrinhas/

The Barreira Megalithic Complex is 1 km (5/8 mi) from the museum. It is located on private land, with limited access. When we visited, the gate was open, so we walked up to the site. To get there: facing away from the museum, turn left on Avenida Prof. Dr. D. Fernando de Almeida, following that road to the left past the bus stop. Stay on the road heading to the Barreira megalithic site, keeping the hill to your left. The gate to the Barreira Megalithic Complex is on the left at the bottom of the hill.

Avenida Prof. Dr. D. Fernando de Almeida
São Miguel de Odrinhas
2705 São João das Lampas
GPS: 38°53'21.9"N, 9°22'18.2"W

Alto da Vigia and Nearby Sites

"I stood near the edge of the cliff, the Atlantic Ocean surging below. To my left, the mist-shrouded slopes of the Mountain of the Moon. To my right, the Colares river flowing into the sea. Before me, the remains of an important Roman temple dedicated to the Sun, the Ocean and the Moon. Millennia ago, this sacred spot marked the western edge of the Roman Empire. Now it is an archaeological dig, its layered secrets—including a medieval Islamic religious building—slowly being revealed." —Elyn

Background

Alto da Vigia is the site of a monumental Roman sanctuary from the 2nd–3rd centuries CE. It was dedicated to the Sun, Moon, and Ocean, and to the Imperial cult*. It included a *temenos* (a sacred precinct), columns, an altar, and various votive inscriptions on stones. The nature of the inscriptions, expressing health to the Emperor and long life to the Empire, indicates that the sanctuary was of significant importance for the Imperial class, not just for private individuals. For example, Sextus Tigidius Perennis, governor of Lusitania, dedicated an inscription to *Soli et Lunae* (Sun and Moon) in 185 CE, and Junius Celanius, another governor, dedicated one between 200 and 209 to *Soli aeterno Lunae* (Eternal Sun and Moon).

The location of the site is quite significant. It is situated at the edge of the Sacred Mountain, the Mountain of the Moon, near Praia das Maçãs (Apple Beach), on an elevated platform with good visibility out to (and from the) sea. To the north is the Colares river, which was navigable until medieval Islamic times and appears to have been used during Roman times. This is a very powerful place, with the sun setting almost directly west into the ocean during the equinoxes. Although nearby Cabo da Roca (see p. 122) is the westernmost location of the Eurasian land mass, it is not easy to access from the sea, nor is it near a (once)navigable river, unlike this site.

Praia das Maçãs/Apple Beach is supposedly named for the prevalence of nearby apple groves, whose fallen fruit drifted down the Colares River and was deposited upon the shore. Luiza Frazão^ draws a fascinating connection between apples (often associated with the Goddess), Avalon/Glastonbury in England, and this part of Portugal. In an interview with Mary Sharratt^ she says, "We believe that the Garden of the Hesperides, like the sacred Island of Avalon, is the dimension of the Goddess in this territory. There is a special physical counterpart of this paradise, which covers Sintra and goes even further north to Ericeira. The entrance portal is at Praia das Maçãs [Beach of Apples]."

The earliest archaeological evidence dates from Roman times, but it is possible that this was a sacred

site long before then. The Romans, like previous and subsequent conquerors, often implanted their temples on places that were sacred to earlier inhabitants. After all, the Alto da Vigia is located on the edge of the Monte da Lua—the Mountain of the Moon—whose ancient reputation for sacredness was well known to the Greeks and Romans.

The "apples of the Hesperides" symbolize immortality. In Roman mythology, apples are associated with Aphrodite/Venus, and apple branches were used in the rites of Diana, whose Moon-goddess associations reverberate in this area. In other words, the seemingly benign "Apple Beach" place-name may be a reference to ancient goddess worship that existed in the region and even, perhaps, at this very site.

Over the centuries, the Roman sanctuary gradually began to disappear, some of its stones carted off for local building activities, others buried under shifting sands. The site was rediscovered in the 16th century. According to one account, in 1505, workmen were ordered by Dom Manuel I to construct a lookout tower at the site. Their shovels encountered three inscribed altars, and they immediately informed the king. He came to visit, bringing with him a Sicilian scholar, Cataldo Sículo, and the courtier Valentim Fernandes, who recorded the visit in several letters.

Cataldo Sículo looked at one of the inscribed altar stones and improvised a neo-Latin epigram proclaiming that it honored the Portuguese empire.

He said it described the prophecy of the Sibyls that the stones would reappear during the Age of Discovery, when "the riches of the Ganges and Indus rivers entered the Tagus." All this, he asserted, was decreed by the Eternal Sun and Moon. Dom Manuel was delighted.

According to José Cardim Ribeiro, the first excavator of the site, the only thing accurate in this statement was the mention of the Sun and the Moon. It was, in other words, a masterful bit of marketing by Sículo, designed to curry royal favor. The king was enthralled, and the false epigram was repeated in 16th- and early 17th-century books, even finding its way into a preface to Nostradamus' prophecies (see Pereira Rosa^).

Just as tourists today flock to see the wonders of Sintra, national and international visitors soon traveled to the site. Miguel da Silva, the future bishop of Viseu, went to visit in 1512 and accurately recorded inscriptions on two of the altar stones; the third was already illegible.

In 1540, Luís, the erudite brother of Dom João III, visited the ruins and brought with him Francisco de Holanda. De Holanda identified the ruins as a Roman sanctuary, making this the first verified archaeological discovery in Portugal. He drew an imaginative reconstruction of the site that included a circle with 16 altars, with a central sun disk and the nearby landscape.

> "Alto da Vigia" refers to a high lookout spot.

In subsequent centuries, the sanctuary disappeared once again. The existence of a Roman temple somewhere near Praia das Maçãs had been documented and continued to be remembered, but finding it was the problem. By the 20th century, sheep grazed over the site and later it became a vineyard. In the last half of the 20th century, ground cover was planted to prevent erosion.

José Cardim Ribeiro (founder and first director of the Archaeological Museum of São Miguel de Odrinhas [see p. 170]) began looking for the Roman sanctuary in the 1980s but missed finding anything substantial, his small, informal survey passing within inches of the then-unknown Islamic precinct. Frustrated but certain there was something to be found, the MASMO archaeology team reexamined the letters of Fernandes and the drawings of de Holanda. His drawings provided some guidance for the location.

They began searching for the sanctuary again. A small hilltop overlooking the beach, known locally as the Alto da Vigia and also as Alconchel, became the focus of their investigation. An archaeology excavation under the direction of Alexandre Gonçalves began in 2008. Much to everyone's surprise, they uncovered the remains of a Moorish *ribat*, a coastal defense post and spiritual retreat for Islamic religious soldiers, constructed sometime before the 12th century. Although long forgotten, a hint of its existence had remained in the Arabic-influenced topographic name of Alconchel (*al-concilium*). A necropolis was also discovered, probably related to the Islamic occupation phase. The remains of a modern-era torchlight watchtower were still visible nearby, additional indication of the importance of the location.

Conducting the dig was arduous and dangerous. Sometimes the archaeologists were secured by harnesses as they worked near the edge of the unstable cliff. Finally, one day a Roman altar was found upside down, reused in the *ribat*. The archaeologists turned it over and read the first line of the inscription: "Sun and Ocean." Eureka! According to Teresa Simões, current MASMO director, this demonstrated without doubt that they had found the Roman sanctuary and that some of its stones had been reused by the Moors (see Pereira Rosa^).

In the following years the team made more finds, including more inscriptions, a lintel, an oratory niche, and other evidence that small buildings coexisted on the hill with the large temple. In all (including stones that were recovered from neighboring gardens and yards), they discovered ten inscribed stones, of which eight were altars. These range from the time of Hadrian (the beginning of the 2nd century CE) to Aurelian or Probus (275–280 CE). The inscriptions suggest that for nearly 150 years animals with specific characteristics were sacrificed at the temple to the Ocean, the Moon, and the Sun. Alto da Vigia contains half of the altar stones dedicated to Oceano that are known from the Roman Empire.

As you walk around the archaeological site, imagine what it might have looked like 2,000 years ago. The sea would have been pounding against the rocks below, the sun would have been setting into the ocean, and the moon would have hidden itself behind the Monte da Lua. Then, as now, this would be the perfect place for a sanctuary dedicated to the Sun, the Moon, and the Ocean.

The 4th-century conversion of the Roman Empire to Christianity meant that pagan practices were forbidden. At Alto da Vigia, far from the center of the empire, polytheistic worship appears to have continued for several centuries. Then, half a millennium later, Moorish invaders constructed living quarters and a mosque on the sacred site. According to some reports, it's possible that in 1109 Viking raiders led by the Norse king Sigurd I encountered the Moors at Alto da Vigia and slaughtered them.

Cardim Ribeiro hopes that future excavations will uncover more inscriptions, votive offerings, and even the circular temple described by de Holanda. Perhaps it wasn't entirely an act of creative imagination on de Holanda's part.

In 2021, the Alto da Vigia Archaeological Site was classified by the Ministry of Culture as a Site of Public Interest. There are plans to develop a visitation route with information panels. The artifacts discovered at Alto da Vigia are on display in the Archaeology Museum of São Miguel de Odrinhas (see p. 170).

Nearby Sites to Explore

Tholos da Praia das Maçãs/Prehistoric Monument of Apple Beach

The nearby Tholos* da Praia das Maçãs (Tholos do Outeiro das Mós) is just across the river to the north of the Alto da Vigia, affirming the lengthy importance of this sacred landscape. It is intervisible with the Tholos do Praia das Maçãs. This suggests an ancient relationship between the two sites. The tholos was discovered in 1927 and declared a National Monument in 1974.

It is the only known tholos* in Iberia associated with an artificial cave that dates from the end of the 4th millennium BCE. It has been thought that the tholos was added to the cave in the 3rd millennium BCE, but some research suggests it was all built in the 4th millennium BCE. The megalithic construction was used for a long time and by different communities, from the Bell Beaker Culture to the Iron Age. Microliths, arrowheads, polished axes, and cylindrical stone idols have been uncovered there. They are displayed in the Lisbon National Museum of Archaeology and Ethnology and in the Regional Museum of Sintra.

The tholos is on a high, sandy knoll, surrounded by housing. Since 2020, it has been undergoing restoration work funded by the Sintra Municipality.

Beaches

Praia Grande is a very pleasant, clean, 2 km (1.25 mi) long sandy beach with beautiful cliffs. As well

as being a popular spot for surfing and bodyboarding, it has another attraction: dinosaur footprints. Some 66 fossilized dinosaur footprints have been found on the southern cliffs, about 50 m (165 ft) up from the sandy beach, which was a mud flat when the footprints were made.

They are 170 million years old and were left by both herbivorous and carnivorous dinosaurs. The most visible ones are on a limestone slab on a slope reached via a 370-step staircase leading up from the south end of the beach. Due to unstable cliffs, the staircase is currently closed.

On the northern side of the beach is a huge saltwater swimming pool, attached to the Arribas Sintra Hotel. It is open May-September and can be accessed for an

entrance fee. The pool is an excellent place to swim with children or when the waves are too intense. The view of the ocean from the Arribas Sintra Hotel restaurant is excellent, as is the menu. There are other cafes and restaurants on the beach as well.

Just south of Praia Grande is Praia da Adraga, listed as one of the most beautiful beaches in Portugal and (in 2003) as one of the top 20 beaches in Europe. It is at the end of an ancient river that over millennia carved a gorge through the dark volcanic rocks. There is a large natural arch at the entrance, created by erosion of the underlying limestone rock.

At low tide you can walk to nearby Praia do Cavalo and, going up the cliff, you can see the Fojo natural crater, also created by limestone erosion. According to Roman legend, the Fojo is the home of a 90-meter-tall Triton who plays a conch shell.

At the southern end of the beach is the immense Pedra de Alvidrar (the "Rock of Reason"). Young men used to show their bravery by climbing it. According to another legend, in Roman times this was a place where the accused would be thrown off the rock. If they survived, they were innocent; if not, the sentence had already been carried out.

There is a good restaurant on the beach. The beach is a 40-minute hike (1.6 km/ 1 mi) from Praia Grande

on the GR11-E9 hiking trail. It is part of the Sintra-Cascais Natural Park.

Getting There/Other Information

To get to the Alto da Vigia you need to go to Praia Grande or Praia das Maçãs, either of which is approximately 11 km (6.8 mi) from Sintra. From Praia Grande or Praia das Maçãs, you walk up a trail to the archaeological site. The trail from Praia das Maçãs requires fording the Colares stream and then hiking up the cliffside. The red-and-white marked trail from Praia Grande runs along the top of the cliff and is easier.

Scotturb buses 440 and 442 go from Sintra to Praia das Maçãs. In summer, a narrow-gauge tourist tram runs from near the Sintra Art Museum (MU.SA) to Praia das Maçãs. The red-line CitySightSeeing bus stops at Praia Grande. Scotturb bus 439 leaves from Portela de Sintra bus terminal (just outside the train station at the stop before Sintra) and takes about 35 minutes to reach Praia Grande. Bus 441 also stops by Praia Grande. Always check the bus website for current schedules.

The easiest way to get to Alto da Vigia is to take a car/Bolt/Uber. If you take a Bolt/Uber, you can ask to be dropped off at the Quinta da Vigia, Rua da Praia Pequena, which is nearer to the Alto da Vigia than Praia Grande. Follow the trail along the top of the cliff to the archaeological dig. An explanatory plaque describes the features of the *ribat* and points out what remains of the Roman sanctuary. There are several restaurants at nearby Praia Grande and Praia das Maçãs.

The Tholos da Praia das Maçãs is located near the tram station, public parking, and the beach in the small town of Praia das Maçãs. It is currently undergoing restoration and may be closed to the public. The address is Travessa Galrão 7, Colares, although it is in the beach town of Praia das Maçãs.

Getting to the Beaches

Buses (see above) go to Praia Grande and Praia das Maçãs. Car/Bolt/Uber/taxi also go there. You can

walk from Praia das Maçãs to Praia Grande to Praia da Adraga.

https://en.wikipedia.org/wiki/
Archaeological_Site_of_Alto_da_Vigia/

Archaeological Site of Alto da Vigia: GPS: 38°49'25"N, 9°28'18"

Tholos: GPS: 38°49'35"N, 9°27'59"W

Capela de São Mamede de Janas/Saint Mammes Chapel

"An unusual round church, possibly built over a Roman temple of Diana. A ritual in which animals are driven three times counterclockwise around the chapel and blessed. That's my kind of powerful place!" —Elyn

Background

São Mamede de Janas has been sacred for a long time. Local legend asserts that there was a temple dedicated to Diana at the site. Prehistoric remains in the vicinity indicate that the importance of this sacred site goes

back even further. The current incarnation of the temple is a round, white-washed chapel located on a sandy rise, 600 m (0.37 mi) up the road from the village of Janas. A small pine forest is behind it, a large clearing in front of it. The chapel has been classified as a Monument of Public Interest since 2014.

Archaeological explorations have discovered numerous Roman artifacts nearby, but much to their surprise, archaeologists were unable to find any vestiges of an early Roman temple under the current chapel. What they thought had been the visible foundations of the temple between the buttresses

turned out to be a ring of stones built to support the current church. The archaeologists did uncover, however, a necropolis under the floor of the chapel. A gravestone in the shape of a Templar cross was also found.

A hermitage to São Mamede (Saint Mammes) was documented at the site in 1494. A chapel at this location had been in existence for some time prior, during the Mozarabic* period, from the 9th to 12th centuries. A piece of charcoal discovered in the baptistry attached to the church dates to the 9th century. Archaeological evidence indicates that an octagonal church may have existed here until the 16th century.

The current building resembles a white dovecote with a red-tiled roof and dates from the late 16th century. Legend (and a Sintra Pastoral Unit postcard from 2013 on sale at the chapel) states that the chapel is modeled after a circular temple of Diana that existed there millennia ago. The 16th-century church was probably designed by Francisco de Holanda, who also designed a much-smaller circular chapel at nearby Quinta da Penha Verde. Was he recreating the ancient circular temple that existed there, or that he thought existed there? Was he creating a new circular temple, based on his affection for the classical circular designs he had seen in Rome? We just don't know.

Or—just possibly—was the 16th–century chapel rebuilt as a circular church because it was based on a medieval Knights Templar* church at that location? A number of Templar churches are circular or octagonal, referring to the Temple of the Dome or the rotunda of the Church of the Holy Sepulcher in Jerusalem. According to Luis Élye^, the Knights Templar were given land in this area in the Middle Ages. And there may have been an octagonal church at this location. We know a gravestone shaped like a Templar cross was discovered in the necropolis. Beyond that, we can only speculate.

The archaeologists created a crypt, a kind of basement, under the chapel. Prior to their intervention in 1989–1990, there was a necropolis under the floor of the church but no crypt. The archaeologists left *in situ* a number of the stone-slab graves, including one still containing a small skeleton, and the Templar gravestone. The crypt can be visited by prior arrangement with the priest.

What we can say without doubt is that the plan of the current chapel is circular, with seating around the circumference and rows of benches lined up in the chapel. On the south, a white-washed porch with a

red-tiled roof extends half-way around the chapel. The porch has two entrances. The meter-high, white-washed, exterior wall of the porch is connected to the roof by stone columns. The small rectangular apse of the church, which holds the high altar, faces east and includes a small bell tower. There are three large external buttresses with rows of rocks between them.

In the center of the circular chapel is an unusual construction that

extends from the floor to the roof. It is a *tempietto*, constructed of a large drum supported on six smooth Italianate columns. It is probably the work of Francisco de Holanda, whose name is also associated with the predecessor to the

archaeology museum at Odrinhas (p. 170) and with the drawing of a circular Roman temple at Alto da Vigia (p. 179).

Our guide told us, "First they built a square chapel here, but it fell down. Then they built a rectangular chapel, but it also fell down. Finally, they built a circular chapel—and it stayed standing!"

Along with its unique appearance and intriguing history, the chapel is also famous for the unusual "Blessing of the Cattle" that takes place on August 17, São Mamede's feast day. Traditionally, cattle were driven three times counter-clockwise around the church. The Sintra Pastoral Group postcard refers to this tradition as "coming from immemorial ages" and the direction as "moonwise," an intriguing reference to Diana's association with the moon.

Often, livestock owners left wax ex-votos* and offerings such as cereals (wheat, barley) and olive oil. At the festival, the owners purchase protective colored ribbons that have been blessed by the priest. They

place them around the necks of their animals—or their own necks, or inside their cars. The animals themselves are also blessed. In the past, livestock were driven to the chapel from as far away as Cascais (24 km/15 mi) and Torres Vedras (55 km/34 mi). Today, the ceremony blesses horses, cows, chickens, rabbits, and pets, and includes music, food, and carnival rides.

> A local resident told us, "We used to tell noisy children they should go three times around São Mamede's. We knew that would calm them down."

Saint Mammes (Mamas) of Caesarea was a teenage Christian martyr, thrown to the lions in approximately 275 CE. Instead of attacking him, the lions listened to him preach, and one became his companion. He is patron of breastfeeding babies and protector of those with broken bones. In Portugal, he is also the protector of livestock.

The Roman goddess Diana was the patron of animals, both wild and domestic. She was also associated with childbirth. Traditionally, the three-day Roman Nemoralia or Festival of the Torches took place from August 13–15 in Diana's honor—quite close to

São Mamede's August 17 feastday. Diana's festival was widely celebrated, and it included tying prayer ribbons and leaving tokens, including dough ex-votos* and fruit, in sacred places. It emphasized Diana's protection of those, including animals, who were in her care.

Although the evidence is circumstantial, it seems possible that the Christian Blessing of the Cattle is a continuation of a much more ancient pagan celebration, and that veneration of the Christian martyr Mamede was substituted for that of the Roman goddess Diana. But we just don't know.

São Mamede Chapel is a case study in the difficulty of knowing what happened in the past—and the danger of trusting what is stated as fact on the internet. Legend associates the place with a circular temple of Diana. But was it? Did the archaeologists simply miss the evidence? And what about the ritual blessing of the animals that are driven three times counterclockwise around the church, animals that really have little to do with São Mamede but more to do with the goddess Diana? What is folklore, what is reinvention of tradition?

Getting There/Other Information

Capela de São Mamede de Janas festival on YouTube: https://www.youtube.com/watch?v=6zmtr5btsmA/

São Mamede de
Janas Festival

Address: Estrada de S. Mamede Janas (on the Janas–Fontanela Road), 2710-286 Sintra

Telephone: (+351) 219 244 744

Open during mass hours. Visits only by booking.

GPS: 38°49'59"N, 9°26'11"W

Penedo and Nearby Sites

"I don't know what to make of it. The location of Penedo is impressive, but its fame rests on the ritual slaughter of a bull during an annual festival. The act reeks of pagan sacrifice, but it was performed during a Christian festival in honor of the Cult of the Empire of the Holy Spirit. This 13th-century utopian cult believed in the coming of an age of peace, justice, and equality."* —Elyn

Background

Penedo is considered one of the most traditional villages—if not *the* most traditional—in Sintra. It winds its way around a high spur (*pena*) of the

Mountain of the Moon, in the middle of the Sintra-Cascais Natural Park. The views are spectacular. Little is known about its foundation, but the village is mentioned as early as the 13th century. Archaeological evidence points to much earlier habitation of the place.

In the center of the village is a large stone cross and an attractive, blue-trimmed, white-plastered fountain. Just up the street is the Capela do Penedo e Nossa Senhora das Mercês/the Chapel of Santo António and Our Lady of Mercy. Originally dedicated to Our Lady of Mercy, the church was constructed in 1547 by Francisco Nunes Dias and his wife, Maria dos Anjos Gonçalves Perpétua.

The interior walls of this simple rural chapel are covered with geometrical blue-and-white tiles, added during renovations conducted around 1628. Narrative tiles depict the life of the popular Franciscan Saint Anthony, who was born in Lisbon in 1195 and died in 1231 in Padua. He was canonized in 1232. He is invoked all over the world as the patron saint for the recovery of lost items—including people, things, and spiritual goods.

Laid in the pavement just inside the church is a gravestone. Legend says that long ago, a lady who had "not led a good life" asked to be buried inside, just in front of the main door. She wanted her body to be trod on by people entering the church. The chapel has been classified a Property of Public Interest since 1961.

What makes Penedo a powerful place is its mountaintop setting and its unusual annual festival.

Penedo is said to be the last place on the Portuguese mainland where the Festas do Divino Espírito Santo are held; they continue to be held in the Azores.

The festivals originated in the Cult of the Empire of the Holy Spirit, a radical utopian belief system that dates to the late 12th century. It was begun by a visionary monk named

Joachim, abbot of a Franciscan monastery in Fiore, Italy, who died in 1202. He thought the third world era, the Era of the Holy Spirit, would begin in 1260, ushering in a time of peace, justice, equality, and brotherly love.

The cult* quickly became popular among intellectuals, including Dante, and aristocrats, many of whom were attracted to its utopian vision. Some followers of the cult reasoned that the organized Church would not be needed after the new Empire arrived. Not surprisingly, the Catholic Church decided the cult was heretical in 1256 and eradicated it in most of Europe by the end of the 13th century. Franciscans and the Knights Templar resisted the condemnation.

The cult continued in Portugal, however, under the auspices of Dom Dinis (1261–1325)—a supporter of the Templars—and his wife, sainted Dona Isabel (1271–1336). The monarchs moderated the cult's more radical elements, founded a church in Alenquer (north of Lisbon) dedicated to the Holy Spirit and staffed by Franciscans, and established a lay brotherhood to organize Festivals of the Holy Spirit, initially on Pentecost (50 days after Easter). Pentecost is the day the Holy Spirit purportedly descended upon the Apostles, causing them to speak in tongues.

The Festa dos Tabuleiros* in Tomar* is also related in origin to the Cult of the Holy Spirit. Tomar was the Portuguese center for the Knights Templar*/Order of Christ, a group that, like the Franciscans, continued to support the Cult of the Holy Spirit long after it was condemned by the Church.

In Penedo, the Festivals of the Holy Spirit traditionally included crowning a child, who represents the

Emperor of the Age of the Holy Spirit, and the *Bodo* (feast), a charitable distribution of food commemorating the feeding the poor miracles associated with Dona Isabel.

At some time in the past, during the festival, an ox would be dragged three times around the church. Later, a bull was substituted for the ox and dragged on a rope through the village. During the festival at São Mamede de Janas (see p. 195), cattle are driven three times around the church and given protective, blessed ribbons at the conclusion of their journey.

At Penedo, on the other hand, after being dragged through the village, the bull was killed by a knife in the jugular and butchered near the fountain. The proximity of water helped with the subsequent cleanup operation. Half the meat was cooked into stew to feed the poor; the other half was sold to provide income for the festival and the church. The public bull slaughter was ended in 1985.

Ritual bull slaughter? That seems pagan, not Christian. There is abundant evidence of bull sacrifice in Roman times. The Roman army spread the Cult of Mithras* throughout the empire; its central rite was the ritual slaughter of a bull with a knife. We know that bulls were sacrificed at nearby Alto da Vigia (see p. 179) during Roman rituals. Before Roman times, the bull was associated with the Goddess and its horns with the Moon. Perhaps the Penedo bull sacrifice harkens back to something much older than Christian festivities in honor of the coming Empire of the Holy Spirit.

Nearby Sites to Explore

Ermida de Nosso Senhor do Rio Velho/Hermitage of Our Lord of Rio Velho and Quinta do Carmo

It's an idyllic setting: an isolated stone chapel built into a vine-covered stone wall, surrounded by giant ferns and lush greenery, located next to the swift-running Rio Velho. Once, this hermitage near Penedo may possibly have been dedicated to Santo Adalberto Drepanense, a saint of the Carmelite order, who lived in the nearby Convento de Sant' Anna do Carmo. The chirping of birds, the babbling stream, the sound of the breeze rustling the leaves in the trees—it is a wonderful, tranquility-restoring place to spend a few hours.

The nearby Quinta do Carmo is the location of the early–16th–century Convento de Sant' Ana, a Carmelite Convent*. After the dissolution of monastic groups in 1834, the convent was purchased and transformed into a private estate. It currently belongs to an American. You can see some of it through the massive metal gate. If you follow the wall surrounding the estate to the Rua do Rio Velho, you can look inside and admire the bell tower, the beautifully maintained buildings, and the elegant gardens. From there, you can walk down to the hermitage.

Getting There/Other Information

Penedo is approximately 10–14 km (6–8.5 mi) from the historic center of Sintra. It is difficult to reach without a car/taxi/Bolt or a bicycle.

Penedo church GPS: 38°47'37.6902"N, 9°27'18.828"W

Penedo is a popular spot for cyclists; the owner of the Refugio do Ciclista was a professional cyclist. His simple, traditional-style restaurant serves reasonably priced, fresh-grilled meat and fish for lunch, and a visit is included in some area adventure and jeep tours.

The Hermitage of Our Lord of the Old River is downhill and east of Penedo. It can be reached by walking down from Penedo on the Caminho da Boca da Mata. Or, you can take Scotturb bus 403 to the bus stop at Avenida Br. Vasc-Quinta Arriaga in Colares and walk up (and down) to the hermitage. It may take half an hour or longer to walk to the hermitage; it's about 1.8 km (1 mi), but much of it is uphill.

The hermitage can also be reached by driving from Colares to Gigarós on N375 and parking there to begin walking. It's possible to continue to drive up the Caminho do Carmo to the Quinta do Carmo, where you may be able to park out of the way of traffic. Be aware that you are surrounded by private property and some of the owners don't like trespassers and object to cars being parked nearby.

Follow the quinta wall to the Rua do Rio Velho and keep walking downhill. After a short distance, the pavement ends and cobblestones begin. The cobblestones soon turn into an uneven medieval (possibly Roman) stone path that leads down to the chapel and the river. If you cross the river and continue up the unpaved road, you will pass several houses on your right and, after climbing further up the road, you will reach Penedo. Be careful: the cobblestones are slippery when wet.

GPS for hermitage: 38°47'31.2"N, 9°26'47.8"W
Address: Caminho do Rio Velho, 2705 Colares

Minas/Mines and Tunnels

"Water dripped from the ceiling and plopped onto the glistening floor. The cramped, crudely excavated limestone cave twisted and turned. Nervously, I wondered what I would encounter around the next curve, beyond reach of the dim electric light that had guided my way up till then. I switched on my smartphone flashlight, just in case." —Elyn

Background

Legends abound of mysterious tunnels honeycombing Sintra Mountain. Some say there is a tunnel that links the Moorish Castle on the hilltop to the

National Palace in the historic center of Sintra, several kilometers away. Others assert that the Knights Templar*, who were gifted much of Sintra by Dom Afonso Henriques in the 12th century, built tunnels under their possessions to provide escape routes if needed because of a siege. Still others claim that a tunnel linked the Capuchos Convent, on the Mountain of the Moon, to the Capuchos Convent 77 km (48 mi) away in Arrábida, on the Mountain of the Sun. Since this tunnel would have required excavating beneath the Tejo/Tagus estuary, it would indeed have been a truly exceptional feat of engineering.

As unlikely as it may seem, there is truth hidden within the legends. There are hundreds of tunnels and *minas* (water mines) throughout the Mountain

of the Moon. The *minas* were constructed to collect and channel water down the mountainside. In some of them, water percolates through the porous limestone into a covered drainage system. Some include reservoirs and cisterns. Although some *minas* are large, most are too small to enter. Many continue to channel water to targeted locations as well as provide a protected environment for bats and insects.

Some of the *minas* probably date back to the Moorish period (9th–12th centuries) and were part of a very sophisticated irrigation system. Others were constructed in the 18th through 20th centuries to bring water to the parks and quintas on the hillsides of the Mountain of the Moon. Dom Fernando II constructed numerous *minas* to provide water to the romantic streams and fountains in Pena Park (see p. 85). Some 70 years later, Carvalho Monteiro required a lot of water for the water features in Quinta da Regaleira (see p. 53), so he purchased a number of *minas*. Rights to the *minas*, like rights to land, were purchased and legalized by deed.

In addition to the *minas*, there are numerous tunnels and at least one aquaduct. Many tunnels are also

minas, but not all *minas* are tunnels. For example, the tunnel that leads from the breakfast room of the Sintra Boutique Hotel is both a tunnel and a *mina*. It is 2 m (6 ft) high. It can be explored for approximately 30 m (100 ft). The end of the tunnel has been blocked off, but water continues to drip from the limestone walls and ceilings, accumulating in a tile drainage channel along one side of the floor.

A tunnel network used to be accessible from beneath Café de Paris, across from the National Palace (see p. 40). It is said that that one tunnel led south to the National Palace and had two branches to the north. One branch led to the nearby Church of San Martin and one (perhaps) to the Moorish Castle. The owners of the café no longer permit exploration. There are numerous tunnels and *minas* in Pena Park as well, but most have been closed off.

Getting There/Other Information

A car or bicycle is the easiest way to access many of these sites. A number of *minas* are visible on either side of the N247-3, between the Chalet of the Countess of Edla and Capuchos Convent. Trails (including mountain-bike trails) through the woodland can be accessed through the two "Tapada de Fonte Velha" entrances. These lead to various *minas*, including a vine-covered, 10 m (33 ft) high aqueduct. *Minas* can also be seen in Monserrate Park, on the way up to the Moorish Castle, in Pena Park, near Capuchos Convent, and en route to the Chapel of Santa Eufemia.

You can experience some atmospheric tunnels by exploring the underground passageways in Quinta

da Regaleira. Some of the tunnels are part of an initiatic journey linked to the Initiatic Well and are open to the public. There are also tunnels at one end of the Lake of the Labyrinth (see p. 61).

Finding other tunnels to explore is problematic. Many have been closed to the public. Search online or, better yet, enlist the help of an excellent licensed local guide like Maria João Martinho^. She can show you where many *minas* are, and she has explored a number of tunnels.

Inaccessible or Difficult to Access Places

We have described a selection of powerful places in Sintra and the Mountain of the Moon. There are many more. Some are on private land and closed to the public. Others require special permission to access. Still others are hidden in the forests or down a dirt trail, and only a knowledgeable and experienced guide can take you there.

Some of these sites include:

Megalithic site on private land at Bela Vista, Colares;

Quinta da Penha Verde, site of the earliest human habitation in the Serra as well as the location of an unusual 16th–century circular chapel;

The Chapel of Melides in Colares, said to have been built near the site of an apparition of the Virgin. She appeared to a small group of Templar knights. She encouraged them to fight the Moors, saying something like, "Go, as if you were a thousand!";

Quinta da Bella Vista, formerly the property of Sir Arthur Conan Doyle, author of the Sherlock Holmes mysteries;

The Eagle and Rabbit Rocks;

Tunnels hidden beneath Quinta da Regaleira;

Tholos da Praia das Maçãs;

Penedo da Saudade in the grounds of Seteais Palace Hotel;

Biester Palace and Park, a 19th–century Romantic-style palace and botanical gardens. Soon to be open to the public.

The enchanted forests...

The more we learn about Sintra, the more we have to learn. We are grateful to live here and to be able to continue to explore this amazing, powerful place.

Appendix—Welcome to Sintra

In September 2021, Gary and I rented an Airbnb in Sintra. We had been living in Évora, in the Alentejo region of Portugal. Évora has a magnificent 2nd–century Temple of Diana and is surrounded by important megalithic sites, but it was too hot to settle there permanently. We needed to move.

We had visited Sintra briefly eight years before, and I remembered its powerful allure—the fairytale palaces, the mist-veiled Mountain of the Moon. We decided to spend a month in the town and determine if we wanted to live there. Our Airbnb was in a quiet location downhill from the historic center, next to a large public parking lot that was always empty at night.

As the sun set and the full moon rose on the eve of the Autumn Equinox, I heard the faint sound of bagpipes wailing in the evening air. Puzzled, I went in search of the source. In the nearby parking lot, a bearded man in a long dark coat was playing the *gaita*, the Portuguese version of Scottish pipes. A woman wearing fringed suede shorts and a halter top danced barefoot in front of him, her back turned toward him, her long dark hair flowing down her back.

She twisted a large hoop around her supple hips, over her head, up and down her arms and back again as she swayed to the music. Sometimes she swung the hoop into the air and caught it; sometimes she shrugged her shoulders and the hoop suddenly stood on end.

Time stood still—or maybe it moved back, back to a time when Sintra was the site of sacred ceremonies dedicated to a moon goddess later known to the Greeks as Cynthia, and later yet as Artemis and Diana.

The *gaita* wailed, the woman danced. Suddenly, she spun her hoop and tossed it over the moon. I gasped.

I knew then that we had to move to Sintra. Sintra had caught me in its magical net and there was no escape. I also knew that we had to write a *Powerful Places in Sintra* guidebook so that we could give voice to the land.

(Based on Elyn's journal notes, 21 September 2021)

Glossary (*)

Al-Andalus: Refers to the Muslim and Arab states ("the Moors") that occupied much of the Iberian Peninsula (modern-day Spain and Portugal) from 711 until the collapse of the Spanish Umayyad dynasty in the early 11th century. Expulsion of the Moors during the Christian Reconquest took place at different times in different areas. In Portugal, the final expulsion came in 1249; in Spain it was in 1492.

Anta: Portuguese for dolmen*.

Apse: In a church, the rounded, semicircular projection from the building, usually at the east end, in which the altar is located.

Armillary sphere: An early astronomical device composed of a series of overlapping rings, with a model of the Earth or the Sun placed in the center. It was used for solving various astronomical problems to a crude degree of accuracy. It is a symbol of Portuguese navigational prowess.

Azulejos: Portuguese and Spanish painted tin-glazed ceramic tilework. Dating back to the Moorish invasion of Iberia, the word *azulejo* stems from Arabic roots, meaning small, polished stone. Tilework became popular in Portugal in the 16th to 17th centuries, on both the inside and outside of buildings.

BCE: Before Common (or Current) Era. It is a more neutral term than BC (Before Christ).

Caminho das Cruzes: See Via Sacra/Way of the Cross*.

Carnation Revolution of 1974: Peaceful coup begun by the Portuguese military but soon coupled with a popular civil resistance campaign. Almost no shots were fired and, during the celebrations marking the end of the Salazar dictatorship, carnations were placed in the muzzles of rifles and on military uniforms.

CE: Common (or Current) Era. It is a more neutral term than AD (After Christ).

Convent: Although "convent" often refers to a house where nuns live in community, it also refers to, as in Capuchos Convent, the residence of a community of mendicant (begging) friars.

Cult: The traditional sense of the word means "accepted religious practice" and is not pejorative.

DOC: Denomination of Controlled Origin—a government awarded, restricted label ensuring the product comes from a specific location.

Dolmen: An ancient megalithic structure composed of large upright stones with a capstone. They are often said to be burial chambers, but many appear to have functioned as seasonal ceremonial sites and may not have been used for burials. They may have served other purposes as well. Many Portuguese antas* or dolmens are 4,000 years old or older.

English garden style: Trees are not planted in lines but in groups; flower beds are replaced with lawns and shrubs; and there is a preoccupation with making the most of carefully calculated views of natural or artificial grottoes and streams. Small buildings, statues, and obelisks are strategically placed. The house becomes an integral part of the garden.

Epigraphic stones: Stones inscribed with writing and symbols. Epigraphers use inscriptions (epigraphs) to study writing styles, clarify meaning, provide dates, classify usage, etc.

Equinox: The time in spring and fall when day and night are the same length. Usually around March 20-21 and September 20-21.

Ex-votos: A votive offering, such as wax or metal body-part replicas, crutches, or framed photos or letters. Offered to a saint or divinity to fulfill a vow, to request assistance to heal from illness or injury, or in gratitude.

Festa dos Tabuleiros (Festival of the Trays) in Tomar: Also known as the Festa do Divino Espirito Santo and dates to the Cult of the Empire of the Holy Spirit. As standardized in 1950, the festival is celebrated every four years and includes the Banner of the Holy Ghost, crowning emperors and kings, very tall headdresses (trays) topped with an armillary sphere or the Dove of the Holy Spirit, and cartloads of bread, meat, and wine, pulled by "the symbolic sacrificial oxen" decorated with gilded horns and ribbons. The sharing of bread and meat by the population is celebrated on the day after the processions.

Gothic style: Architectural style popular from the 12th to at least the 16th centuries in Europe, evolved out of Romanesque*. Characterized by thinner walls, supported by flying buttresses, large stained-glass windows, pointed arches and windows, rib vaults, and ornate decoration. Gothic cathedrals seem to soar to Heaven.

Green Man: A sculptural form composed of a human-like face or mask surrounded with greenery or composed of leaves. Often vines sprout from its mouth, nose, and sometimes from its eyes. It is thought to represent an ancient nature deity and symbolizes cycles of rebirth, new growth, etc. It is found world wide.

Guardians of the land or place: Refers to the "spirits of place," the energies of the land itself. Imagine that the land itself has unseen residents who inhabit a specific location, much like you inhabit your home. Just as you wouldn't enter someone's home without asking permission, it is advisable to ask permission before entering powerful places/spaces in nature. For example, you may notice two boulders or two trees with a path between them, that indicate an energetic boundary for the place you are about to enter—something like a "private property" sign.

Knights Templar: The Poor Fellow-Soldiers of Christ and of the Temple of Solomon was a Catholic military order founded in 1119. Its members took vows of poverty. They were initially headquartered on the Temple Mount in Jerusalem and, over a period of two centuries, the order became extremely wealthy and powerful. On Friday, October 13, 1307, King Phillip IV of France ordered the Grand Master and other Templars to be arrested. Under pressure from the king, Pope Clement issued a papal bull ordering European kings to arrest Templars and seize their assets. The arrested knights were tried for heresy. In 1312 the Pope disbanded the order and turned over their assets to the Knights Hospitallers.

Knights of Christ: In Portugal, Dom Dinis I refused to persecute the Knights Templar*, but in 1312 he had to go along with their dissolution by the pope. Rather than arresting them, Dom Dinis sent the Portuguese Templars to the south of Portugal. In 1319 he rebranded them as the newly established Military Order of Knights of Christ. The Knights of Christ, based in Tomar*, inherited the Portuguese Templar assets, property, and personnel. In 1789, Dona Maria I secularized the order. In 1910, with the end of the Portuguese monarchy, the order was extinguished. It was revived in 1917 as an honorific order, conferred as a decoration for outstanding service to the State.

Leprosy: In the Middle Ages and later, a number of different skin diseases were often given the name leprosy.

Luís Vaz de Camões: Lived approx. 1524-5–1580. Considered Portugal's and the Portuguese language's most important poet. He has been compared to Shakespeare, Homer, and Dante. His most important poem, first published in 1572, is *Os Lusíadas (The Lusiads)*. It is one of the greatest epic poems of the Renaissance, immortalizing Portugal's voyages of discovery. Central to the narrative is Vasco da Gama's pioneer voyage via southern Africa to India in 1497–98.

Lunation: A crescent-shaped artifact.

Manueline style: Refers to a sumptuous, composite, elaborate architectural style developed between 1490–1520, during the reign of Dom Manuel I. Maritime elements and references to the Voyages of Discovery predominate in a mix of many other art styles. It includes references to the sea, maritime and botanical motifs, twisted strands of rope, Christian references, armillary spheres, and much more.

Master Builders: A guild of designers and builders of medieval buildings, especially churches and cathedrals, who knew how to locate and construct these buildings according to specific ratios and astronomical orientations. Some of the principles and techniques they used have been rediscovered in recent times and are once again being taught, under the labels of sacred geometry, geomancy, and Zahori arts.

Mithras, Mithraic Mysteries: Possibly based on the Zoroastrian/Iranian Mithras, god of light, the Mithraic Mysteries were developed during the Roman Empire and very popular with the Imperial army from the 1st to 4th centuries CE. Central to the cult was the image of Mithras slaying a sacred bull with a knife. Ritual reenactments took place in an underground temple called a *mithraeum* and were followed by a ritual supper.

Mozarabic: Refers to Iberian Christians, including Christianized Iberian Jews, who lived under Muslim rule in Al-Andalus after the Christian Visigothic Kingdom was conquered by the Umayyad Caliphate, which invaded Iberia in 711. Although they remained Christian, they adopted Arabic language and culture.

Mudejar: Medieval art style influenced by Islamic art but produced typically by Christian craftsmen for Christian patrons. Application of decorative Islamic art motifs and patterning, including calligraphy, intricate geometry, and vegetal forms.

Neo-Mudejar: A more recent art style based on Mudejar.

Pena/penha: Hilltop, rock, or crag. High point on a mountain.

Reconquest/Reconquista: Refers to the lengthy effort by Christian forces to reconquer the Iberian Peninsula after the 711 Moorish invasion from North Africa. The Moors were gradually pushed back by expanding Christian states. The Moors were expelled from Portugal in 1249. The Spanish Reconquista ended with the fall of the Nasrid kingdom of Granada in 1492.

Renaissance style: Popular in Europe beginning in the 14th–16th centuries, it was based on a conscious revival and development of classical architecture, with emphasis on ancient Roman design. It focused on symmetry, harmony, geometry, proportion, and balance. It features hemispherical domes, semi-circular arches, orderly rows of columns and pilasters, and numerous niches.

Ribat: An Arabic term for a small fortification built along a frontier to house military volunteers who fought to defend Islam.

Romanesque style: A medieval European architectural style that began between the 8th–11th centuries, depending on the country. Characterized by massive stone and brickwork, thick walls, semi-circular arches, barrel-vaulted ceilings, small windows, and (in churches) lots of figurative sculpture, some of which is bizarre or even humorous.

Sea stacks: Isolated outcrops of rock standing in the ocean, separate from the land. They are remnants of rocky headlands that have been eroded by wave action.

Sephardic: From the Hebrew *Sefarad*, meaning Spain. Sephardic Jews, also known as (plural) Sephardim, originated from communities that had settled in the Iberian Peninsula from at least the later centuries of the Roman Empire until their expulsion in the 15th century. The term also sometimes refers to Mizrahi Jews of Western Asia and North Africa.

Serra: A mountain range.

Solstice: The summer solstice is the time when the day is longest and the night shortest, usually around June 21. Midsummer Night and the Eve of St. John the Baptist are also celebrated at that time. The winter solstice is the time when the night is longest and the day shortest, usually around December 22. Christmas is celebrated close to that day.

Syenite: A coarse-grained, intrusive igneous rock similar to granite but deficient in quartz.

Telluric currents: Natural electric or energy currents that move underground or through the sea.

Tholos: An ancient megalithic structure composed of a central chamber topped with a false dome, somewhat like a beehive, and partially dug into the ground. Thought to be group burial chambers, they began appearing in Portugal approximately 4,500 years ago. Some tholos were re-used during the later Bronze Age.

Tomar: Center of the Knights Templar* in Portugal; later the center for the Military Order of Christ, which succeeded the Knights Templar. See Festa dos Tabuleiros*.

Via Sacra/Way of the Cross: A contemplative Catholic practice, in which a route is marked with 14 stations that recount the events on the day Jesus was crucified. The faithful walk the path during Lent, especially on Good Friday.

Bibliography and Guides (^)

Adrião, Vitor Manuel. *Quinta da Regaleira* (Sintra, História e Tradição). Lisbon, Portugal: Dinapress, 2013.

Andersen, Hans Christian. *A Visit to Portugal 1866*. 1st Edition, English Translation. Bobbs-Merrill, 1973.

Anes, José Manuel. Interview on "Quinta da Regaleira, the Mysteries and Initiations." *Sintra News*, May 19, 2017. https://sintranoticias.pt/2017/05/19/jose-manuel-anes-quinta-da-regaleira-os-misterios-as-iniciacoes/

Boim, Miguel. *Sintra Lendária—Histórias e Lendas do Monte da Lua*. 3rd Edition. Sintra, Portugal: Zefiro, 2021.

Bueno Ramírez, Primitiva, and Jorge A. Soler Díaz. *Ídolos—Miradas Milenarias, Guia Catálogo*. Madrid: Consejo de Administración Museo Arqueológico Regional de la Comunidad de Madrid, 2020.

Byron, George Gordon (Lord Byron). *Childe Harold's Pilgrimage*. First published between 1812-1818. Mentions Cintra (Sintra) in the First Canto.

Cardim Ribeiro, José. "Soli Aeterno Lunae—Cultos Astrais em Época Pré-Romana e Romana Na Área de Influéncia da Serra de Sintra: Um Caso Complexo de Sincretismo?" In *Diis Deabusque, Actas do II Colóquio Internacional de Epigrafia, "Culto E Sociedade," Sintra, 1995*. Sintra: Museu Arqueológico de São Miguel de Odrinhas, pp. 595-624.

Camões, Luís Vaz de. *The Lusiads*. Originally published in 1572. London: Penguin Classics, 1981.

Capote Gonçalves, José. *O Cabo da Roca*. Leiria, Portugal: Hora de Ler, 2019.

Cardoso, João Luís. *Territórios da Pré-História em Portugal Lisboa e Estremadura*, Vol. 6.2. Tomar, Portugal: CEIPHAR, 2006.

Cunha, Rodrigo. *O Colar de Sintra*. Serra de Sintra: Castelo do Amor, 2016.

Élye, Luis. Geometer, fine artist, teacher of sacred geometry, and esoteric guide. Contact at Elyegeometria@gmail.com and https://www.geometriasagrada.pt/

Frazão, Luiza. *A Deusa do Jardim das Hespérides—Desvelando a Dimensão Encoberta do Sagrado Feminino em Portugal*. 2nd Edition. Sintra, Portugal: Zefiro, 2021.

Fielding, Henry. *Journal of a Voyage to Lisbon. 1754*. Various editions.

Jack, Malcom. *Sintra—A Glorious Eden*. UK: Carcanet Press Ltd, 2002.

King's Chronicler. "Sintra e a sua Historia" Sintra, Portugal, Câmara Municipal de Sintra. https://en.wikipedia.org/wiki/ Sintra. And https://web.archive.org/web/20110807005808/ http:/www.cm-sintra.pt/Artigo.aspx?ID=3383

Martinho, Maria João. Excellent, very knowledgeable guide for the Sintra region, tunnels, Templar history, etc. Leads jeep and walking tours. Contact at martinhosintra@gmail.com or https://www.facebook.com/martinhosintra

Martins, Rui. *A Mensagem Alquímica da Quinta da Regaleira*. (No publishing data.)

Pena, António, Luís Goes, and José Cabral. *Sintra—A Borough in the Wild*. Câmara Municipal de Sintra, n.d.

Pereira, Denise, Paulo Pereira, José Anes. *Quinta da Regaleira—história, símbolo e mito*. Sintra: Fundação Cultursintra, n.d.

Pereira, Paulo, José Guapo, Manuel F. Chaves, and Paula Benito. *Portugal Megalítico*. Lisbon: Edições Inapa, 2008.

Pereira, Rosa, Gonçalo. "The enigmatic site of Alto da Vigia in Praia das Maçãs." *National Geographic,* October 10, 2021. https://nationalgeographic.pt/historia/grandes-reportagens/2327-o-enigmatico-sitio-do-alto-da-vigia

Quinta da Regaleira. Boxed set of booklets, available at the Quinta gift shop. www.cultursintra.pt.

Sapina Gussing, Anjos. "The enigmatic site of Alto da Vigia." https://nationalgeographic.pt/historia/grandes-reportagens/2327-o-enigmatico-sitio-do-alto-da-vigia

Sharrat, Mary. "The Goddess in Portugal." July 9, 2021. https://feminismandreligion.com/2021/07/09/the-goddess-in-portugal/

Silva, Freddy. *First Templar Nation*, Revised Edition. Rochester, Vermont: Destiny Books, 2017.

Sintra I–II (Tomo 1), 1982–1983. Gabinete de Estudos de Arqueologia, Arte e Etnografia, Museu Regional de Sintra—Museu Arqueológico de São Miguel de Odrinhas. Cámara Municipal de Sintra, 1984–1987.

Vieira da Silva, José Custódio. *The National Palace, Sintra*. London: IPPAR and Scala Publ. Ltd., 2002.

Index

D

Author Biographies

Elyn Aviva, Ph.D., M.Div., is a transformational traveler, writer, and fiber artist. Her Ph.D. in anthropology was on the contemporary Camino de Santiago pilgrimage. She first walked the 500-mile-long route across northern Spain in 1982. Elyn has written numerous books on pilgrimage, spiritual quest, and powerful places, as well as several novels. For a number of years, she has explored western esoteric traditions, Kabbalah, sacred geometry, shamanic practices, active dreaming, and non-physical healing modalities. To learn about Elyn's fiber art, go to www.fiberalchemy.com.

Gary White, Ph.D., is a retired Distinguished Professor of Music Theory and Composition, an award-winning composer, and a textbook author. He is also an accomplished dowser and seasoned traveler through the interface between this world and the imaginal realms. With Elyn, he is co-author of "Powerful Places Guidebooks." Gary is responsible for the design and production of Pilgrims Process publications and for hosting the Powerful Places podcasts and Transformative Travel interviews posted on his Youtube channel, https://www.youtube.com/user/tchbth/videos/

Elyn and Gary grew up in the midwest of the US, moved to Spain in 2009, and then to Portugal in 2021. They have walked the Camino de Santiago pilgrimage route from Saint Jean Pied de Port across Spain, from Santiago de Compostela to Finisterre, and from Le Puy-en-Velay in France. They have studied with several geomancers and dowsers, including Dominique Susani, Ferran Blasco, Anne Zonne Parker, and Sig Lonegren. Elyn and Gary are avid explorers of our fascinating, multidimensional universe. They are grateful for the guidance they have been given that has led them to where they are.

To learn more about Elyn and Gary's publications, go to www.pilgrimsprocess.com and www.powerfulplaces.com. To read some of Elyn's articles, go to www.YourLifeIsATrip.com/home/author/elynaviva/ or do a search for Elyn Aviva or Gary White on https://Ancient-Origins.net